Today,

GOD WANTS YOU TO KNOW

Inspiration for a Woman's Soul

BARBOUR
PUBLISHING

Cover and interior design by Kirk DouPonce, dogeareddesign.com

Published by Barbour Publishing, Inc., P.O. Box 719, Uhrichsville, Ohio 44683, www.barbourbooks.com

Our mission is to publish and distribute inspirational products offering exceptional value and biblical encouragement to the masses.

Member of the
Evangelical Christian
Publishers Association

Printed in India.

Introduction

Today, God Wants You to Know. . .

Y ou're a wonder woman, balancing every area of your life—
home, work, ministry. . .the list goes on. The hours are long,
but the days are still too short to get everything accomplished. And
time spent with your heavenly Father is usually the one thing that is
left unchecked on your daily to-do list.

The Father knows what it is to be busy, and He understands
the stress we feel when our schedules are bursting at the seams.
Even when we don't take the time to hear His voice, He's still
there—encouraging and supporting us every step of the way.

These encouraging devotional readings come to you straight
from the Father Himself. Make it a priority to meet Him every day
in His Word, through a devotional thought, and in prayer. Even on
the days you feel like you don't have a second to spare, dedicate a
few minutes to let Him know what's on your heart. He'll bless the
rest of your day immeasurably. That's a promise you can count on.

The Publishers

Today, God Wants You to Know…
He Is Faithful

I pray that God, the source of hope, will fill you completely
with joy and peace because you trust in him. Then you will
overflow with confident hope through the power of the Holy Spirit.
ROMANS 15:13 NLT

In our busy, fast-paced lives, we may feel exhausted at times. Our culture fosters frenzy and ignores the need for rest and restoration. Constantly putting out fires and completing tasks, working incessantly, we may feel discouraged and disheartened with life. There is more to life than this, isn't there?

Our God of hope says, *"Yes!"* God desires to fill us to the brim with joy and peace. But to receive this gladness, rest, and tranquillity, we need to have faith in the God who is trustworthy and who says, "Anything is possible if a person believes" (Mark 9:23 NLT). We need to place our confidence in God, who, in His timing and through us, will complete that task, mend that relationship, or do whatever it is we need. The key to receiving and living a life of hope, joy, and peace is recounting God's faithfulness out loud, quietly in your heart, and to others. When you begin to feel discouraged, exhausted, and at the end of your rope, *stop*; go before the throne of grace and recall God's faithfulness.

God of hope, I recount Your faithfulness to me. Please fill me with Your
joy and peace, because I believe You are able to accomplish all things.
Amen.

Today, God Wants You to Know...
the Comfort of a Friend

The heartfelt counsel of a friend
is as sweet as perfume and incense.
PROVERBS 27:9 NLT

When you think of the word *comfort*, what comes to mind? Maybe it's a favorite pair of jeans or a well-worn sweatshirt. It might be chocolate or homemade mac-and-cheese—foods that soothe in a difficult time. Or perhaps it's a luxurious bubble bath, complete with candles and relaxing music.

While all these things can bring temporary relief, God's Word tells us that finding true comfort is as simple as sharing a heart-to-heart with a friend. Whether it's over coffee, dessert, or even on the phone, a cherished friend can offer the encouragement and God-directed counsel we all need from time to time.

Friendships that have Christ as their center are wonderful relationships blessed by the Father. Through the timely, godly advice these friends offer, God speaks to us, showering us with comfort that is as sweet as perfume and incense. So what are you waiting for? Make a date with a friend and share the sweet aroma of Jesus!

Jesus, Your friendship means the world to me. I value the close friendships You've blessed me with, too! Thank You for the special women in my life. Show me every day how to be a blessing to them, just as they are to me.

Words Can Be a Blessing

Let your conversation be always full of grace, seasoned with salt,
so that you may know how to answer everyone.
COLOSSIANS 4:6 NIV

Inflection. Tone of voice. Attitude. Maybe you remember your
mom saying, "It's not what you say but how you say it." Words
not only convey a message; they also reveal the attitude of our
hearts. When our conversation is full of grace, even difficult truths
can be communicated effectively. But how do we season our words
with grace?

Grace is undeserved favor that extends unconditional love to
another. Whether you're communicating with friends, family, or
coworkers, it's important to show that you value them. Put their
needs above your own. Communicate truth within the context of
love. Show compassion and forgiveness. Demonstrate understanding
and an openness to receive their input. Respect their opinion. Rather
than striving to drive home your point, try to understand theirs. Seek
to build them up. Convey encouragement and hope. Be positive.

When our conversations are full of grace, people will enjoy
communicating with us. They will walk away blessed by the love
we have shown. Today, in your conversations, extend God's grace to
those hungry to experience His love.

Dear Lord, may I view each conversation as an opportunity to
extend Your grace to others. May my words be a blessing. Amen.

There Is a Purpose

*"My righteous ones will live by faith. But I will
take no pleasure in anyone who turns away."*
HEBREWS 10:38 NLT

We clean the windows and wash the car, and a day later it rains. We sweep the kitchen floor, and hours later the crunch of cookie crumbs resounds under our feet. Some tasks seem so futile.

So it is with our spiritual life. We pray unceasingly and no answers seem to come, or we work tirelessly and problems entrench us. In frustration we wonder, *Why did this happen? What purpose is there to all of this?* It all seems so pointless.

To the skeptic, logic must pervade every situation. If not, there is no basis for belief. But to the person of faith, logic gives way to faith—especially during the most tumultuous, nonsensical times.

So even when our prayers remain unanswered, we continue to pray. Even when God is silent, we continue to believe. And though we grope for answers, we continue to trust.

When our chaotic lives turn upside down and we labor to find rhyme and reason, God asks us to hold fast to our faith. For no labor of love is pointless; no prayer is futile.

*Dear Lord, please forgive me for allowing my problems to undermine
my faith. I trust in You, knowing that my faith in You is never futile.
Amen.*

Today, God Wants You to Know...
His Favor

And so find favor and high esteem in the sight of God and man.
PROVERBS 3:4 NKJV

When God laid out the blueprint for building your life, He scheduled the right people in the right places at precisely the right times for every phase of your life. He provided favor, lined up doors of opportunity, and arranged for perfect connections to help you construct a great life. God's blessings have already been ordered and are placed precisely throughout your journey called life.

But now it's up to you to recognize the opportunities and meet each appointment God has for you. You must walk by faith, listening to His direction and instruction so you can be quick to experience every good and perfect gift He has for you. God wants you to experience every favor and rich blessing He's prepared. By faith, expect blessing to meet you at every turn.

Imagine what your future holds when you become determined to step out to greet it according to God's design. Remain alert and attentive to what God wants to add to your life. Expect the goodness He has planned for you—doors of opportunities are opening for you today!

Lord, thank You for setting favor and blessing in my path,
and help me to expect it wherever I go and in whatever I do. Amen.

Today, God Wants You to Know...
His Forgiveness

Let us test and examine our ways, and return to the LORD!
LAMENTATIONS 3:40 ESV

What if you could follow yourself around for the day, carefully examining all that you do? Look at your schedule—your choice of activities, the people you talk to, the things you listen to and watch, the habits being formed, the thoughts you think. Maybe your heart desires intimacy with God, but a real day in your life leaves no time for solitude. God often speaks to us in the stillness and in silent spaces. How will we hear Him if we're never still?

Taking time to reflect, to think, and to examine oneself is a necessary step in moving toward intimacy with God. Before we can turn back to Him, we must repent of the things that moved us away from Him in the first place. As we set aside time for solitude and reflection, the Holy Spirit will gently show us these things if we ask. He will show us the sins we need to confess and give us the grace of repentance. Experiencing forgiveness, we find that our fellowship with our heavenly Father is restored.

Lord, help me to still myself before You and be willing to examine my ways. Speak to me through Your Holy Spirit about what is wrong in my life. Give me the gift of repentance and allow me to enjoy the sweetness of Your forgiveness.

Today, God Wants You to Know...
the Joy of Sharing His Love

Let no corrupt communication proceed out of your mouth, but that which is good to the use of edifying, that it may minister grace unto the hearers.
EPHESIANS 4:29 KJV

A coffee filter serves an important role in the brewing of a fine cup of coffee. It holds back the bitter grounds while allowing the soothing, aromatic drops of rich coffee to flow into the pot. When you remove the filter, it contains nothing but soggy, dirty coffee grounds that no longer serve any good purpose.

Imagine what would be found if a filter were placed over your mouth to capture all that is distasteful before it left your lips. How full would that filter become before the day ended?

Our Father desires that our words be soothing and inspiring, never bitter or distasteful. In fact, His message of love cannot flow from a bitter mouth. We can ask the Holy Spirit to be our filter in order to keep the bitter grounds out of the tasty brew that God intends to come forth from our mouths. With the filter of the Holy Spirit in place, He can use us to bring His message of love to those around us.

Heavenly Father, please forgive my harsh and bitter words of the past. Help me to use a fresh filter on my tongue each day so I may bring Your comfort and joy to those whose lives I touch. Amen.

Today, God Wants You to Know...
Complete God-Confidence

> *If my people, who are called by my name, will humble*
> *themselves and pray and seek my face...then I will hear from*
> *heaven, and I will forgive their sin and will heal their land.*
> 2 CHRONICLES 7:14 NIV

Some people consider humility a weakness. Others think humility means never talking about yourself or always putting yourself and your accomplishments down. Christians often confuse humility with low self-esteem, believing we should not think of ourselves as worthy, because Jesus Christ was the only perfect person.

But when we accept Christ as our Lord and Savior, His life becomes ours. We are no longer slaves to sin, but we own His righteousness. So we don't have to go around thinking that we're scum.

Our Savior walked in total God-confidence—knowing that His steps were planned—and He had only to listen to His Father's heartbeat to know which way to go. He could withstand insults, persecutions, and dim-witted disciples because He knew who He was and where He was headed.

Today, live in total God-confidence, knowing you'll be able to withstand the pressures life throws at you, because He is your life.

> *Father God, I praise You for Your forgiveness and healing.*
> *Thank You that I am called by Your name.*

the Blessings of Obedience

The LORD came and stood there, calling as at the other times, "Samuel! Samuel!" Then Samuel said, "Speak, for your servant is listening."
1 SAMUEL 3:10 NIV

The Lord spoke—*out loud*—to the young boy Samuel. Although this incident happened thousands of years ago, Samuel's response teaches us important lessons today. The boy viewed himself as God's servant and revealed a heart that was committed to obedience. Maybe that's why the Lord chose to speak to this youngster.

Although the Lord's call today is different than in Old Testament times, He still speaks to hearts that yearn to listen. The Lord speaks powerfully through His Word, the Bible. The Holy Spirit also whispers truth to our hearts. Even other people and His creation may reveal God's message to us.

The Lord most often communicates to servant hearts that are ready to listen—hearts committed to obedience. Servant hearts trust that God's ways are best even when they might be difficult. They covet His counsel and seek His voice.

The Lord longs to communicate with us. Is your heart receptive to His call today? Work toward being able to say sincerely, "Speak, Lord, your servant is listening!"

Dear Lord, may I have a servant's heart that's committed to obedience. Speak, Lord! Amen.

Today, God Wants You to Know. . .
the Importance of Persistence

*"For the past twenty-three years. . .the LORD has been giving
me his messages. I have faithfully passed them on to you."*
JEREMIAH 25:3 NLT

The Bible is full of persistent people, people who persevered despite problems and difficulties, long after the time most people would consider such persistence wise. Noah spent one hundred years building the ark. Abraham waited twenty-five years for Isaac, the son of promise. And by the end of his life, Jeremiah had preached God's message to an unbelieving audience for forty years. Israelites called him a traitor, threw him in prison, and left him to die, but he continued preaching God's message. Nothing slowed him down.

Jeremiah's faith enabled him to persevere. The writer of Hebrews could have had Jeremiah in mind when he wrote, "Still others were chained and put in prison. . . . They went about. . .destitute, persecuted and mistreated—the world was not worthy of them" (Hebrews 11:36–38 NIV).

God expects the same persistence of us. He calls for persistence, also known as perseverance, over a dozen times in the New Testament. He means for the trials that come our way to increase our perseverance. When we successfully pass small hurdles, He may put bigger ones in our way. Why? Because He doesn't love us? No—because He does.

Persistence results in faith that is pure, molten gold.

*Lord, we can only persist because You are unchanging.
We pray that we will keep our eyes fixed on You and keep moving
forward, regardless of what happens around us. Amen.*

Today, God Wants You to Know...
He Knows Your Heart

We are not trying to please people but God, who tests our hearts.
1 Thessalonians 2:4 niv

Much of what we say and do stems from our desire to be accepted by others. We strive to make a certain impression, to shed the best light possible on ourselves. Wanting to be viewed as successful, we may decide to exaggerate, embellish, or even lie. It's difficult to be true to ourselves when we care so much about the acceptance and opinions of others. Impression management is hard work, so it's good to know God has a better plan!

Rather than being driven by the opinions of others, strive to live your life for God alone and to please Him above all else. God knows our hearts. He perceives things as they truly are. We cannot fool Him. When we allow ourselves to be real before Him, it doesn't matter what others think. If the God of the universe has accepted us, then who cares about someone else's opinion?

It is impossible to please both God and man. We must make a choice. Man looks at the outward appearance, but God looks at the heart. Align your heart with His. Let go of impression management that focuses on outward appearance. Receive God's unconditional love and enjoy the freedom to be yourself before Him!

Dear Lord, may I live for You alone. Help me transition from being a people pleaser to being a God pleaser. Amen.

Today, God Wants You to Know...
You Can Always Trust Him

Hear my prayer, O LORD, and let my cry come to You.
PSALM 102:1 NKJV

Have you had days when your prayers seemed to hit the ceiling and bounce back? Does God seem distant for no reason you're aware of? Chances are good that if you've been a Christian for more than a short time, you've experienced this.

The psalmist experienced it as pain and suffering became his lot. At night insomnia plagued him. During his tired days, enemies taunted him. His was a weary life, and in earthly terms, he hardly could see the outcome.

But once the psalmist described his plight, his psalm turned in a new direction, glorifying God. Suddenly, life wasn't so bad anymore because he trusted in the One who would save him.

When prayer hits the ceiling, it's time to remind ourselves of God's greatness, not complain about what we think He hasn't done. As we face trials that threaten to undo us, let's remind ourselves that He has not forgotten us and that our ultimate security is never at risk.

As we feel the dangers of life, let's trust that God is still listening to our prayers. He will never fail us. All He asks is that our reliance on Him remains firm. At the right hour, we'll feel His love again.

Even when I don't feel Your presence, Lord, You have not deserted me.
Keep me trusting and following You, O Lord. Amen.

Today, God Wants You to Know...
He Cherishes One-on-One Time with You

Then the cloud covered the tabernacle of meeting,
and the glory of the LORD filled the tabernacle.
EXODUS 40:34 NKJV

God wants us to enter worship with a heart prepared to actually meet Him. He longs for us to come in the frame of mind where we're not just singing about Him, but truly worshipping Him with every fiber of our being. He wants wholehearted participants, not spectators.

God promises to meet with us. When we come into His presence, if our hearts and minds are truly engaged, He often overwhelms us with His goodness, His greatness, His Word. Think about the last time you truly "engaged" God—met with Him in a supernatural way. Has it been awhile?

It's the Lord's desire that we come into His presence regularly, not in an "I have to get this over with" frame of mind, but with a "Lord, I am so blessed to get to spend time with You!" attitude. When we meet with Him in that mind-set, the shining greatness of the Lord will be revealed, and His glory will fill that place.

Lord, I long to meet with You—really meet with You. I don't want to
go through the motions, heavenly Father. I want Your glory to fall,
Your shining greatness to overwhelm me. Today I offer myself to You,
not as a spectator, but as a participant in Your holy presence.

17

Today, God Wants You to Know...
Who You Are in Him

For if you listen to the word and don't obey,
it is like glancing at your face in a mirror. You see yourself,
walk away, and forget what you look like.
JAMES 1:23–24 NLT

Are you real? There are many reasons people wear masks and refuse to become completely transparent even with those they consider their closest friends.

It's so wonderful to find people who can be real with us. We are drawn to them because they are genuine and true—never pretending. Such boldness and confidence come with knowing who we are in Christ. As we trust Him to help us, we examine our lives and then learn to shape them to reflect the goodness of God.

It is a process. We begin by looking into the mirror to see what we need to remove of the old person we used to be so that we can take on the character and nature of God.

Too often, we miss the value of sharing our failings. We don't want to be vulnerable, so we hold back. In doing so, we deprive others of who God created each of us to be. When you share from your own experience—especially your failures—you increase empathy, you're more approachable, and you increase your "relatability" to others. Let your guard down and be all you were created to be.

Lord, help me to be real with those You have put around me. I pray
that they see You through me and it draws them closer to You. Amen.

Today, God Wants You to Know...
He's Available

I have no regrets. I couldn't be more sure of my ground—
the One I've trusted in can take care of what he's trusted me to do.
2 TIMOTHY 1:11–12 MSG

Ever feel like giving up? Throwing in the towel? Some days it's hard to find the resolve to persevere. Despite our human frailties, our heavenly Father is there to grab our hands and pull us to our feet. He isn't impressed with what we do in life but with how we tackle each day. He wants us to gaze at Him and know He's there to take care of us despite the overwhelming odds life brings.

Paul could have given in. The man was shipwrecked, beaten, imprisoned, and persecuted, and yet he kept on giving the Lord praise. He preached the good news of Jesus and faced the consequences of his actions. Few of us will face the same persecution, but we have the same Spirit within us that Paul did. He told Timothy he had no regrets because he was sure of the One he served.

Are you sure today of the One you serve? When coming to grips with difficulties, do you turn to the Creator of the universe and ask for help? You should. He's available. Just reach out and take His hand. He'll be there.

Lord, teach me Your love. Let me feel Your embrace.
I choose to trust in You. Amen.

19

Joy Comes from Him

And even though you do not see [Jesus] now, you believe in him and are filled with an inexpressible and glorious joy, for you are receiving the end result of your faith, the salvation of your souls.
1 PETER 1:8–9 NIV

As children we find joy in the smallest things: a rose in bloom, a ladybug at rest, the circles a pebble makes when dropped in water. Then somewhere between pigtails and pantyhose, our joy wanes and eventually evaporates in the desert of difficulties.

But when we find Jesus, "all things become new" as the Bible promises, and once again we view the world through a child's eyes. Excitedly, we experience the "inexpressible and glorious joy" that salvation brings.

We learn that God's joy isn't based on our circumstances; rather, its roots begin with the seed of God's Word planted in our hearts. Suddenly our hearts spill over with joy, knowing that God loves and forgives us and that He is in complete control of our lives. We have joy because we know this world is not our permanent home and a mansion awaits us in glory.

Joy comes as a result of whom we trust, not what we have. Joy is Jesus.

Dear Jesus, thank You for giving me the joy of my salvation. Knowing You surpasses anything and everything else the world offers. Never allow the joy in my heart to evaporate in the desert of difficulties. Amen.

Hope Is All around You

Why, my soul, are you downcast? Why so disturbed within me?
Put your hope in God, for I will yet praise him, my Savior and my God.
PSALM 42:5 NIV

If you've ever been depressed, you're not alone. Depression can be caused by circumstances, biology, environment, or a combination of all of those things. Research indicates that as many as 25 percent of Americans suffer from depression at some point in their lives.

We are blessed with scriptural accounts of godly people like David and Jeremiah who struggled with depression. These stories let us know that it's a normal human reaction to feel overcome by the difficulties of life.

While feeling this way is normal, it doesn't have to be the norm. As Christians, we have hope. Hope that our circumstances will not always be the way they are right now. Hope that no matter how dismal the world situation seems to be, God wins in the end. Hope that eternity is just on the other side.

Hope is like a little green shoot poking up through hard, cracked ground. When you're depressed, do what David and Jeremiah did—pour out your heart to God. Seek help from a trusted friend or godly counselor.

Look for hope. It's all around you, and it's yours for the taking.

Father, even when I am depressed, You are still God. Help me to find a ray of hope in the midst of dark circumstances. Amen.

Today, God Wants You to Know...

the Beauty of Putting Someone Else First

Love from the center of who you are; don't fake it.
Run for dear life from evil; hold on for dear life to good.
Be good friends who love deeply; practice playing second fiddle.
ROMANS 12:9–10 MSG

The call to love in Romans 12:9–10 is extremely difficult to put into practice. Sure, it's easy to love friends and family, but how easy is it to love that person at school or at work when you just can't relate to her? Being polite is one thing, but truly loving that person is much harder.

Paul tells us that we should not fake love. God says we sin against Him when we *pretend* to love others but dislike them. Instead we are called to *genuine* love.

The Message uses the metaphor "practice playing second fiddle" to help us understand how we are to honor one another. In a musical ensemble, the first fiddle typically plays the melody and all the fancy runs. The second fiddle performs the supporting role, harmonizing with the first fiddle, and acting as the musical anchor. We should always take the second part, putting others before ourselves and encouraging them with all our love and devotion. When we love without hypocrisy and honor others above ourselves, we will live in beautiful harmony with one another.

Dear Lord, please help me to love with a genuine heart
and to take second place to those around me. Amen.

Today, God Wants You to Know...
He Loves You—No Matter What

"For the mountains may depart and the hills be removed, but my steadfast love shall not depart from you, and my covenant of peace shall not be removed," says the LORD, who has compassion on you.
ISAIAH 54:10 ESV

Mountains are steadfast and immovable. Even small parts of mountains are not easily moved. Nature's forces take centuries or tremendous energy to do so. Snow, glacial ice, mountain streams, rain, and wind move one grain of sand or pebble at a time. Volcanoes release tremendous energy to alter a mountain's shape. When man wants to build a highway through a mountain range, the power of dynamite is needed to cut tunnels through rock, and the road must twist and turn to adapt to the terrain.

God says His love is even more immovable. Mountains will move before His love will leave us. Hills will depart more easily than God would remove His covenant of peace with us. In the sacrifice of Christ on the cross, He demonstrated His amazing love for us, and Jesus became our peace. Romans 5:1 (ESV) says, "Therefore, since we have been justified by faith, we have peace with God through our Lord Jesus Christ." Regardless of what we have done or will do, God's love is set upon us. By faith, we have only to believe what Jesus has done for us.

Father, thank You for Your immovable love, for the permanence of Your covenant of peace, and for my righteousness, which does not come from my good works but from Christ's sacrifice for me.

Today, God Wants You to Know...
He Hears Your Prayers

I call on you, my God, for you will answer me;
turn your ear to me and hear my prayer.
Psalm 17:6 niv

No one is available to take your call at this time, so leave a message and we will return your call—or not—if we feel like it. . .and only between the hours of 4:00 and 4:30 p.m. Thank you for calling. Have a super day!

We've all felt the frustration of that black hole called voice mail. It is rare to reach a real, honest-to-goodness, breathing human being the first time we dial a telephone number.

Fortunately, our God is always available. He can be reached at any hour of the day or night and every day of the year—including weekends and holidays! When we pray, we don't have to worry about disconnections, hang ups, or poor reception. We will never be put on hold or our prayers diverted to another department. The Bible assures us that God is eager to hear our petitions and that He welcomes our prayers of thanksgiving. The psalmist David wrote of God's response to those who put their trust in Him: "He will call upon me, and I will answer him" (Psalm 91:15 niv). David had great confidence that God would hear his prayers. And we can, too!

Dear Lord, thank You for always being there for me. Whether I am
on a mountaintop and just want to praise Your name or I am in
need of Your comfort and encouragement, I can count on You. Amen.

Today, God Wants You to Know...
Your Beauty Shines from Within

Don't be concerned about the outward beauty of fancy hairstyles,
expensive jewelry, or beautiful clothes. You should clothe yourselves
instead with the beauty that comes from within, the unfading beauty
of a gentle and quiet spirit, which is so precious to God.
1 PETER 3:3–4 NLT

Fashion gurus love to tell women what to wear. Many like to recommend one pair of red shoes—preferably sassy high heels—to spice up a lady's wardrobe. Proponents of the advice say having one special pair of shoes to wear when feeling down or depressed can turn a woman's whole day around, making her feel beautiful and powerful.

While fashion trends are fun and we all want to look well groomed, we can't forget where true beauty and power come from. Wasn't it Jesus who taught us not to place our treasure in physical things like our bodies or worry about where our clothes will come from? He promises to provide for us.

Shoes scuff, necklaces break, and fabrics fade, but true beauty starts from within. When we allow God to dress our spirits in robes of love, joy, peace, patience, kindness, goodness, faithfulness, gentleness, and self-control, our inner beauty will far outshine anything we put on our physical bodies.

Dear Father, I want to be a woman whose inner beauty
far surpasses my outer beauty, so that when people see
me they are pointed to You and rejoice in Your creation.

You Can Begin Anew

Because of the LORD's great love we are not consumed, for his compas-
sions never fail. They are new every morning; great is your faithfulness.
LAMENTATIONS 3:22–23 NIV

What's the first thing you do when you get up in the morning? Hop on the treadmill? Stumble to the kitchen for a mug of fresh-brewed caffeine? Walk blindly to the bathroom, not opening your eyes until a jet of hot water jolts you awake?

God starts out His day offering renewed compassion to His children. No matter what trials, difficulties, and sins yesterday brought, the morning ushers in a fresh experience, a brand-new beginning for believers who seek His forgiveness. All you have to do is accept the gift.

Are you burdened from yesterday's stress? Are the worries of tomorrow keeping you awake at night? Consider the dawning of the day as an opportunity to begin anew with our heavenly Father. Seek Him in the morning through studying His Word and through prayer, embracing His compassion to be a blessing to others throughout your day.

Father, Your promise of never-ending compassion for me is amazing!
I never want to take for granted the grace You offer every day.
I'm so undeserving, but still You give and give and give. Please help
me to show mercy to others the same way You do to me. Amen.

Today, God Wants You to Know. . .
He Is Working—in His Time

> *"This vision is for a future time. It describes the end,*
> *and it will be fulfilled. If it seems slow in coming, wait patiently,*
> *for it will surely take place. It will not be delayed."*
> HABAKKUK 2:3 NLT

Ah, patience. It's the stuff frustration is made of. And yet it's a virtue the Lord expects His people to have plenty of.

In this fast-paced world, we want what we want and we want it *now*. We don't want to have to wait. And we don't have to—for most things. Microwaves speed up the cooking process. Fast-food restaurants hand us our food as we zip through the drive-thru. Internet access gives us instant access to people, places, and things all over the world. And cell phones give us the chance to connect with folks in a hurry.

Oh, if only we could learn the value of slowing down—of waiting in God's presence. Take another look at today's scripture. Sometimes the things we're waiting on come slowly. Similarly, God's plans may come slowly, but they come steadily, surely. God is going to do what He says He'll do. We don't know when, exactly, but we can be found faithful while we're waiting.

What are you waiting on today? Is your patience wearing thin? Apply the "slowly, steadily, surely" principle and watch God work—in His time.

Lord, I'm used to things moving really fast. And yet I find
myself in a waiting season. Give me patience, Lord, and remind
me daily that Your timetable is the only one that matters.

Today, God Wants You to Know...
He Will Drive "the Foxes" Away

Catch for us the foxes, the little foxes that ruin the vineyards.
SONG OF SOLOMON 2:15 NIV

What makes you fume? You know, those bothersome little annoyances that drive you up the wall? We all have them—like losing our keys when we're in a hurry, missing the train home from work, or losing five pounds only to gain back six over the weekend.

The Bible teaches that the "little foxes" in life "spoil the vine." The real joy-robbers aren't the big catastrophes but the trivial, petty annoyances we encounter daily. One or two consecutive foxes have been known to hurl the best of us into an all-out tailspin, ruining an otherwise perfect day.

So how do we harness little foxes? The psalmist said, "When anxiety was great within me, your consolation brought joy to my soul" (Psalm 94:19 NIV). God understands our human frailty. Wherever we are, whatever we are doing, He is eager to administer calm, peace, and joy! As we turn to the Lord in prayer and praise, He begins to "catch for us the foxes."

God's antidote to our flailing emotions is simple: prayer plus praise equals peace.

Still fuming?

Dear God, please give comfort to my disquieted soul and drive away the little foxes of aggravation. When I'm tempted to fret and fume, remind me of Your antidote to keep my emotions in balance. Amen.

He First Loved You

But if anyone loves God, he is known by God.

1 CORINTHIANS 8:3 ESV

How do we show that we love God? Is it by church attendance? Giving? Doing good deeds? Prayer? These may be manifestations of our love for God, or they may be things we do out of a sense of duty; but loving God is first and foremost a response to being known and loved by God. We can't muster emotion or feeling toward God, nor do we love Him simply by willing ourselves to perform acts of obedience. We begin to love God when we grasp what it means to be known by God.

He knit us together in our mothers' wombs.

He knows the number of hairs on our heads.

He accepts us as we are because of Christ's sacrifice for us.

He has compassion for our weakness.

He forgives our sins.

He longs to commune with us.

He delights to hear our prayers.

He desires to help us, strengthen us, and bless us.

He has given us the Holy Spirit as our comforter, our helper, and our teacher.

He wills all this for us before we ever turn to Him in repentance. We need to reacquaint ourselves with the gospel often, to meditate on what Christ has done for us, and to remember that He first loved us.

Lord, renew my love for You. Help me to remember that
You knew me and loved me before I ever knew You.

He Expects Your Very Best

*Work willingly at whatever you do, as though you
were working for the Lord rather than for people.*
COLOSSIANS 3:23 NLT

Some people pride themselves in being procrastinators. Maybe they enjoy the rush of adrenaline when deadlines loom and the sense of accomplishment when a project is completed at the last minute. Sometimes laziness lies at the root of procrastination— laziness that God says is a sin.

What if Jesus had been a procrastinator? Miraculous healing, earth-rocking teaching, and servant leadership could have taken a backseat to the distractions of the day. Instead of avoiding the un-pleasant parts of His ministry, Jesus took the initiative to live each day to the fullest by completing the plans the Father had for Him.

Today, focus on the tasks at hand. Whether it's in your career, at home, at church, or at school, give your all. After all, Jesus didn't put off the job; He came to earth to complete His Father's will by dying on the cross for our sins. He deserves our very best, not tomorrow—today.

*Jesus, please forgive me when I don't always do my best.
Help me to always remember Your example of hard work and
follow-through during Your earthly ministry. In this way—
and many others—I want to be like You. Amen.*

the Gift of His Grace

"Then neither do I condemn you," Jesus declared.
"Go now and leave your life of sin."
JOHN 8:11 NIV

John 8 paints one of the most beautiful portraits of grace in all of scripture. The woman was dragged from the bedroom and paraded before the men in the temple courts. Can you imagine the humiliation? The man who had likely declared his love for her only moments before was nowhere to be seen. Only the woman was dragged into the temple—already tried and declared guilty of adultery. It was all over except for the stoning.

Until Jesus stepped in. He didn't say anything for what probably seemed like an eternity. Then, "If any one of you is without sin, let him be the first to throw a stone at her" (John 8:7 NIV). With that one sentence, the crowd dispersed. The only man on earth qualified to stone this woman offered grace.

The Pharisees knew the letter of the law like the backs of their hands: adultery meant stoning. But in His gentle and loving way, Jesus brought to light the spirit of the law. Sin begins in the heart. Oh, what freedom is found in the Spirit!

Now, Jesus didn't let this woman off the hook; sin is sin. But under the Spirit, condemnation is no longer necessary. Just a cleansed heart—filled with grace and gratitude for the gift of freedom and forgiveness.

Jesus, thank You that I am not condemned. Thank You that I am forgiven. Free. Help me to live a life of purity to honor You. Amen.

Today, God Wants You to Know...
You Can Rest in Him

But Jesus often withdrew to lonely places and prayed.
LUKE 5:16 NIV

Christians often make the mistake of believing the Lord wants us to be busy about His work constantly. We sign up for everything and feel guilty saying no to anything that is asked of us. This is perhaps especially true of women. We feel it is our duty to serve.

Certainly, we are called to be about God's work. We are His hands and feet in this world, and He can use us in mighty ways. But we are also called to rest and pray. Jesus put a priority on this, frequently leaving the crowd to seek solitude. He encouraged His followers to do the same. One day when they had been busy meeting the needs of people all day, Christ insisted that the disciples come away with Him to rest and to nourish themselves.

There is no denying that our lives are busy. All sorts of demands are placed on women today. You may find yourself in a station in life that pulls at you from every angle. Make time to rest. Find a place that is quiet where you can pray. Jesus modeled this for us. He wants us to find rest in Him.

Father, show me the importance of rest. Allow me to say no to something today in order that I might say yes to some quiet time with You. Amen.

Today, God Wants You to Know...
He Is Your Helper

For I, the Lord your God, hold your right hand;
it is I who say to you, "Fear not, I am the one who helps you."
ISAIAH 41:13 ESV

We shake hands to greet each other; it's a sign of welcome. We reach for the hand of a child when we're walking in a crowd or near a street; it helps protect and comfort the child. In times of great emotion or anticipation, we grab the hand of a nearby friend or family member; it says, "I am with you." By a hospital bed, we clasp the hand of a sick loved one; our hand tells them we are present, suffering with them. With every gripping of another's hand, we are bearing witness to God.

He holds your hand. He welcomes you into His kingdom. He protects you. He comforts you. He is with you in your most anxious moments and in your darkest hours. With the clasp of His hand comes courage for any situation. He tells you not to fear, for He is your ever-present help in times of trouble. He has ahold of you.

Almighty God, I am grateful that You hold my hand.
Forgive me for the times I have forgotten this and let
fear reign in my life. Help me to remember I am never alone.
Grant me the courage that comes from knowing You as my helper.

He Cares about Your Health

*Our bodies. . .were made for the Lord,
and the Lord cares about our bodies.*
1 CORINTHIANS 6:13 NLT

L ate nights. Early mornings. Caffeine. Stress. Overeating.
    All of us have a tendency to burn the candle at both ends.
Today's fast-paced society makes taking good care of ourselves
seem like a luxury.

However, God's Word tells us that if we belong to the Lord,
our bodies are not our own. He lives in us, and we are, in fact, a
temple of the Most High God! He cares about how we take care
of—or neglect—ourselves.

With that in mind, we need to consider how our daily choices
affect our temple. Are you stressed? Take deep breaths and discover
things that reduce your anxiety level. Do your food choices leave
much to be desired? Meet with a nutritionist and discover how
good food can taste—and how good it can make you feel. Is your
only exercise jogging to the fridge for a late-night snack? Do some
stretches or go for a walk.

This week, be aware of how you rest, work, eat, move, and play.
As you move and breathe more mindfully, you'll begin to sense
what things are beneficial to your overall health and to the mainte-
nance of your body—God's temple.

*God, thank You for the gift of my body.
Help me be a good steward of that gift.*

He Longs to Hear Your Praise

I bless GOD every chance I get; my lungs expand with his praise.
PSALM 34:1 MSG

We humans are a self-centered bunch. Even those of us who have a personal relationship with the Creator often neglect to give Him the praise that He deserves. Instead, we choose to focus on our own problems and selfish desires. If we try to place praise high on our list of priorities, it's often difficult to follow through; praise isn't something that comes naturally to most of us.

So how can we develop a spirit of praise every day? First, amp up the amount of time you spend in prayer. As you go throughout your daily routine, find new reasons to offer thanks to the Father: the refreshment of a hot shower, a job to do, coworkers to interact with, food to satisfy hunger, the smile of a friend, the change of seasons. . .the list is endless!

Next, sprinkle your conversations with the hope that your faith gives. Verbally acknowledge God's goodness and provision in your life and in the lives of others. Call a coincidence what it really is— the hand of the Father. Don't be afraid to let your newfound praise bubble over to every area of your life!

Father, You are my God, my almighty Redeemer and Friend!
I praise You because of the wonderful things You do in my life every day.
I praise You for being You! Let everything within me praise the Lord!

Today, God Wants You to Know...
How to Love

Jesus replied: "Love the Lord your God with all your heart and with all your soul and with all your mind.' This is the first and greatest commandment. And the second is like it: 'Love your neighbor as yourself.'"
MATTHEW 22:37–39 NIV

Christians have been given two assignments: love God and love each other.

People say love is a decision. Sounds simple enough, right? The fact is that telling others we love them and showing that love are two very different realities. Let's face it—some people are harder to love than others. Even loving and serving God can seem easier on a less stressful day.

Think about convenience stores. They're everywhere. Why? Because along the journey people need things. It's nearly impossible to take a long road trip without stopping. Whether it's gas to fill our vehicles, a quick snack, or a drink to quench our thirst, everyone needs something. Gas station owners realize this—and we should, too.

It may not always be convenient to love God when the to-do list stretches on forever or when a friend asks us for a favor that takes more time than we want to give. But God's love is available 24/7. He never puts us on hold or doles out love in rationed amounts. He never takes a day off, and His love is plentiful.

Lord, I promise to love You and my neighbor with my whole heart. Amen.

Today, God Wants You to Know...
His Eternal Love

The Lord bless thee, and keep thee: the Lord make
his face shine upon thee, and be gracious unto thee.
Numbers 6:24–25 kjv

Once we have a relationship with God the Father through Jesus Christ, we are in line for a multitude of blessings. Billy Graham said, "Think of the blessings we so easily take for granted: life itself; preservation from danger; every bit of health we enjoy; every hour of liberty; the ability to see, to hear, to speak, to think—and to imagine all this comes from the hand of God." Without realizing it, we were blessed when we opened our eyes this morning. Some of us can add friends, family, freedom, and possessions to that blessing list.

Why do we not recognize all of our blessings? Because it's human nature to zero in on what's wrong and miss what's very right. We overcome that habit through praise of God and fellowship with Him. When we bless God in faithful praise and He blesses us, the result is a renewed strength for daily living.

God's love for us is eternal, as are His gifts. We need to open our arms and become thankful recipients of all He's given. Praise Him and bless His holy name.

Lord, You have given me so much, and I am thankful.
Let me give thanks for Your gifts. Amen.

Today, God Wants You to Know...
He's Busy Working behind the Scenes

Now faith is confidence in what we hope for
and assurance about what we do not see.
HEBREWS 11:1 NIV

Movies, theater, and sports productions all require people working behind the scenes. The audience very seldom sees what it takes to bring the final product together. Hours of preparation, planning, and technical assimilation come together before an audience sees a single performance—the outcome of the production company's hard work.

In the same way, your faith works behind the scenes of your life to produce a God-inspired outcome to situations you face. What you see is *not* what you get when you walk by faith.

Be encouraged today that no matter what takes place in the natural—what you see with your eyes—it doesn't have to be the final outcome of your situation. If you've asked God for something, then you can trust that He is working out all the details behind the scenes.

What you see right now, how you feel, is not a picture of what your faith is producing. Your faith is active, and God is busy working to make all things come together and benefit you.

Heavenly Father, what I see today is not what I'm going to get.
Thank You for working behind the scenes to bring
about the very best for my life. Amen.

Today, God Wants You to Know. . .
He Keeps His Promises

*Moses summoned all the Israelites and said to them, "You have seen
with your own eyes everything the LORD did. . . . For forty years I led
you through the wilderness, yet your clothes and sandals did not wear
out. . .so you would know that he is the LORD your God."*
DEUTERONOMY 29:2–6 NLT

Each election season, political candidates tickle the ears of
listeners by vowing to take care of their constituents. One
promises to cut taxes. Another promises to fix health care and give
the middle class relief.

But there is a graveyard where political promises typically go to
die. When in office, many politicians get distracted by lobbyists or
their party's leaders. And we are disappointed again.

Still, it's our duty and privilege as citizens to vote. But whether
we line up with the conservative or liberal side of politics, we must
not trust in government—or any politician—to save us. Jesus Christ
is the only Savior. And He never breaks any of His promises.

When the children of Israel suffered under their Egyptian
oppressors, God freed them with signs and wonders. Then for
forty years they wandered in the desert, and each day they had just
enough food and water to sustain them.

God will do the same for us. He will clothe, feed, shelter, and
rescue us from those who try to oppress us. What government
can't—or won't—do, God will. Put your trust in Him.

*Lord, thank You that You promise to take care of us.
Help us not to put too much trust in leaders or agencies.*

Today, God Wants You to Know...
He Never Changes

To everything there is a season,
a time for every purpose under heaven.
ECCLESIASTES 3:1 NKJV

Change is a regular part of modern life, as routine as an afternoon thunderstorm—and often just as messy. Jobs shift or disappear. Friends move. Babies are born, and children graduate and marry. On top of lives already crammed to the brim with responsibilities and stress, change comes to all of us.

Only one thing in our lives never changes: God. When our world swirls and threatens to shift out of control, we can know that God is never surprised, never caught off guard by anything that happens. Just as He guided David through dark nights and Joseph through his time in prison, God can show us a secure way through any difficulty. He can turn the roughest times to good. Just as He supported His servants in times past, He will always be with us, watching and loving.

Lord, help me remember Your love and guidance when my life turns
upside down. Grant me wisdom for the journey and hope for the future.
Amen.

His Comfort

> *All praise to God, the Father of our Lord Jesus Christ. God is our*
> *merciful Father and the source of all comfort. He comforts us in all*
> *our troubles so that we can comfort others. When they are troubled,*
> *we will be able to give them the same comfort God has given us.*
>
> 2 CORINTHIANS 1:3–4 NLT

Comfort is often associated with couches and cushions, leather seats of luxury automobiles, and mattresses that adjust to fit the contours of our bodies. There is comfort food like chicken potpie, potato soup, and mac-and-cheese.

If you have ever suffered a loss or an unbearable hurt in your life, then you know the deeper meaning of the word *comfort*. You needed it, and hopefully you received it.

God is the greatest source of comfort for the human spirit. God listens. He provides. At times, you can almost feel His hand stroking your brow as He blesses you with sleep after many sleepless nights.

As God comforts us, we can comfort others. We particularly ought to reach out to others who are facing a challenge we have faced ourselves. There is something about the empathetic comfort of someone who has been in our situation that means even more than the sympathy of someone who hasn't experienced it.

Is there someone in your life who could use some comfort? Offer it in any small way that you are able. The God of comfort has comforted you. So comfort others in His name.

> *Merciful Father, comfort me in my times of need*
> *and show me those whom I might comfort. Amen.*

There Is Strength in Stillness

Be still, and know that I am God: I will be exalted
among the heathen, I will be exalted in the earth.
PSALM 46:10 KJV

The radio plays in the car. The TV blares in the house. Phones ring in both places. The computer delivers e-mail and instant messages. Text messages beep on a handheld device. Our modern world rarely allows quiet. Our society rushes from one thing to the next. For many people, stillness and quiet don't happen until they fall asleep.

Yet God says He is known in stillness. In Isaiah 30:15 (KJV) we read, "In returning and rest shall ye be saved; in quietness and in confidence shall be your strength." God says stillness is good for us. It is how we come to know Him and gain our strength from Him.

He is the Creator of the universe. He makes each twenty-four-hour day. He rules the sun and the moon, the day and the night. He knows every sparrow that falls to the ground. He never slumbers nor sleeps. We can trust Him with the moments of our lives. We can make time for solitude and trust Him to order our day. We can trust Him to meet us in the pause. He is God, so we can be still.

Father, help me today to be still before You.
Enable me to trust You with the cares of my life.

Today, God Wants You to Know...

You Will Be Rewarded for Your Patience

The Lord is good to those whose hope is in him, to the one who seeks him;
it is good to wait quietly for the salvation of the LORD.
LAMENTATIONS 3:25–26 NIV

Life provides all of us with wait training—waiting in line, waiting for traffic, waiting to hear about a new job, waiting for a medical report from the lab. Patience is more than a virtue in today's hypersonic world—it is an essential survival tool for a happy life. And we have so many opportunities to practice it, we should be really good at it by now! But we seldom are. We want answers *now*.

Scripture records that miracles unfold on God's timetable, not ours. Sarah at a baby shower, pregnant in her nineties. David hiding in a cave, waiting to become king. Paul exhorts us in Hebrews to run with endurance and stamina even when we don't immediately see results. God's hand is at work in our lives when we are totally surrendered to His clock. He longs for His children to quit fretting and just wait patiently.

Today, let's choose to give up our rights and yield to God's calendar. The rewards will be great. His Word promises it.

Dear Father, I'm not good at waiting patiently.
Help me learn to lean on You. Amen.

Today, God Wants You to Know...
He Is Right by Your Side

The LORD God Almighty will be with you, just as you say he is.
AMOS 5:14 NIV

Sometimes we have trouble feeling God's presence, especially in troublesome situations. In those times, we may ask, "Where are You, God?"

God has told us that He will never leave us nor forsake us (see Deuteronomy 31:6). So if we feel as if God is not near, perhaps the distance is of our own choosing.

We need to believe God is always with us (see Matthew 28:20). We need to have the knowledge firmly implanted upon our heart, soul, and mind that when we seek Him, He is near.

God warns us, "My people are destroyed from lack of knowledge" (Hosea 4:6 NIV). How true that is! The destroyer revels in the idea of us moving away from God, becoming unfamiliar with Him. The evil one celebrates when we abstain from reading God's Word, praying, and praising Him.

Each day, tell yourself the truth: that God is always with you. Then He "will be with you, just as you say he is."

And during those times when you feel as if God's presence has slipped out of your life, take a look around. See where you are standing. Then make your move. Look into the goodness of His Word. Seek His face. Don't let Him out of your sight. Proclaim that He is standing there, right by your side. And there He will be, just as you have said.

Thank You, Lord, for always being with me.
With You by my side, I will live! I will not be destroyed.
I will overcome all. Thank You for being immovable. Amen.

Today, God Wants You to Know...
You Are His Daughter

So in Christ Jesus you are all children of God through faith.
GALATIANS 3:26 NIV

Galatians 3:26–29 is packed with statements about who you are as a Christian. You are Abraham's seed. You are an heir according to God's promise. And best of all, you are a *child of God*. Galatians reminds us that there is no male or female, race, or social status in the Lord's eyes. Believers are truly *one in Christ*.

You may have had a wonderful upbringing with loving parents. Or you may not have been so fortunate. You may have spent years in the foster system or had abusive parents.

Whether your childhood reflected love or abandonment, there is good news! As a Christian, you are a daughter of the King of kings, the Lord of lords, the sovereign God. He is the One who hung the stars in the sky, and yet He knows the number of hairs on your head. You are not just God's friend or distant relative. You are His *daughter*!

If you have a child of your own, consider the unconditional love you feel for him or her. As intense as that love is, because you are human, you are limited in your ability to love. In contrast, God loves us in a way we will not fully understand until we reach heaven. He is our Abba Father, our "Daddy."

Thank You, Father, for adopting me through Christ as Your daughter.
Teach me to live as a reflection of my Father's love. Amen.

Today, God Wants You to Know. . .
His Light Will Shine on the Best Path

So the cloud of the LORD was over the tabernacle by day,
and fire was in the cloud by night, in the sight of
all the Israelites during all their travels.
EXODUS 40:38 NIV

Have you ever been forced to choose between "good" and "best"? When life presents us with more than one great opportunity, it can be hard to decide what to do. The path we should take depends on many different factors, and the road may not be clear at first.

How do we determine God's will? It's an age-old question, and to be sure, discovering God's choice for us is not easy. But it *is* simple. First, we must pray for God's guidance. He promises to give us wisdom when we ask for it. Second, we need to search His Word and make sure our potential decision lines up with scripture. Third, we should ask for counsel from godly advisers. And fourth, we must search our hearts to see if the opportunity fits well with the personality, talents, and priorities God has given us.

Rest assured, God *will* shine His light on the right path, just as He led the Israelites with a cloud by day and a fire by night. And when it comes, His guidance will be accompanied with peace, joy, and a certainty that we have followed the One who has our (and His) best interests at heart.

Faithful Father, I praise You for Your compassion and concern for me.
Guide me with Your holy light as I seek Your will for my life.

Today, God Wants You to Know...
He Has the Perfect Solution

That clinches it—help's coming, an answer's on the way,
everything's going to work out.
PSALM 20:6 MSG

Have you ever found yourself in need of rescuing? Been so far down in the pit that you wondered if anyone even heard your cries? Maybe you looked for answers but couldn't seem to find them. Perhaps you exhausted every resource. Oh, there's such wonderful news for you today! God has an answer for any problem you face. *Any* problem, big or small. Help is coming; the answer's on the way. Everything is going to work out.

So what do you do while waiting for that answer? How do you deal with problems when they look like they couldn't possibly work out? Trust Him. Sounds easy, but it's tough when you're facing the unknown without clear answers. Still, God longs for you to remain faithful during these times, to remember help really is coming.

If you're going through a particularly stressful time, if you need answers and they don't seem to be coming, recommit yourself to trusting God. Don't try to figure things out on your own. Instead, trust in the King of kings, the Lord of lords, the One who created you and has the perfect solution.

Lord, this whole trust thing is hard when I can't seem to find the answers I need. Today I recommit myself to trusting—not in myself or my answers—but in You. Thank You, Father, that an answer is on its way.

Today, God Wants You to Know. . .
You *Are* because He *Is*

And God said unto Moses, I AM THAT I AM: and he said, Thus shalt
thou say unto the children of Israel, I AM hath sent me unto you.
EXODUS 3:14 KJV

Some women work themselves into a frenzy about the many
things they have to do. Others moan about the tasks they are
unable to get done, while yet others fret over what they still need
to do. The woman who constantly lives with past regrets and future
anxieties can be quite unpleasant in the present.

God is not like this. He doesn't regret or fret. Although He
existed in eternity past and will be in eternity future, God is neither
past nor future. His most revered name is I Am. God is eternally
present.

God *is*. Women *are*. And women are what they are, where they
are, and how they are because God *is*.

Life is not about doing. Life is about who we are in relationship to who God is.

God's first call to us is to Himself, not to His service. "Come
unto me, all ye that labour and are heavy laden, and I will give you
rest," Jesus said (Matthew 11:28 KJV).

Be the woman God wants you to be—rest in Him.

Oh Father, I want to accomplish so much in my life, but sometimes
I'm so busy that I don't have time for You or for others.
Teach me to rest in You, to be all that You want me to be. Amen.

Today, God Wants You to Know...
He's Already Connected and Waiting

The prayer of a righteous person is powerful and effective.
JAMES 5:16 NIV

We communicate with others in our cyberspace world at lightning speed—an e-mail, instant message, or text message—all of these provide quick results. But prayer is even faster than the digital world. We have God's attention the moment we focus on Him.

The concept of the power of prayer is familiar, but sometimes we forget what it means. Prayer is a powerful tool for communicating with God, an opportunity to commune with the Creator of the universe. Prayer is not something to be taken lightly or used infrequently. Yet in the rush of daily life, we often lose sight of God's presence. Instead of turning to Him for guidance and comfort, we depend on our own resources.

But prayer isn't just a way to seek protection and guidance; it's how we develop a deeper relationship with our heavenly Father. We can access this power anywhere. We don't need a Wi-Fi hot spot or a high-speed modem. We just need to look up. He's connected and waiting.

Father, thank You for being at my side all the time.
Help me to turn to You instantly, in need and in praise. Amen.

You Belong to Him

You were bought at a price.
1 CORINTHIANS 6:20 NIV

Sometimes life can feel like a huge puzzle, and we're constantly trying to figure out how our piece of life fits into the big picture. We all have a desire to belong to something special—someone important. Surprisingly, we can overlook the most important connection we have: we belong to God.

No matter where you've been or what you've done, God has accepted you. He is all about your future, and that includes spending eternity with Him. He shaped you to the perfect size to fit into His purpose and plan. And no matter what road you take, He has made a place for you. He purchased you with the price of His own Son's life. And He gave you everything you need to be accepted as a joint heir with Jesus.

When it seems others do not want you on their team or you find you're having a hard time fitting in, remember you are part of God's family—born of the household of faith. He created you and formed you to be a perfect fit.

Heavenly Father, thank You for paying the ultimate price for me to be a part of Your family. When I'm tempted to feel rejected or unwanted, remind me that I don't have to look far to find my perfect place in You. Amen.

He Is the Giver of All Good Things

He restoreth my soul: he leadeth me in the
paths of righteousness for his name's sake.
PSALM 23:3 KJV

Sometimes we become discouraged with the direction of our lives. Circumstances are not of our choosing, not the plan we laid out. God's timetable isn't meshing with ours. But to keep others around us pacified, we paste on a smile and trudge through the murky waters.

Be encouraged. The Lord has promised He hears our pleas and knows our situations. He will never leave us. Our God is not a God of negativity, but of possibility. He will guide us through our difficulties and beyond them. In *Streams in the Desert*, Mrs. Charles E. Cowman states, "Every misfortune, every failure, every loss may be transformed. God has the power to transform all misfortunes into 'God-sends.' "

Today we should turn our thoughts and prayers toward Him. Focus on a hymn or a praise song and play it in your mind. Praise chases away the doldrums and tips our lips up in a smile. With a renewed spirit of optimism and hope we can thank the Giver of all things good. Thankfulness to the Father can turn our plastic smiles into real ones, and as the psalm states, our souls will be restored.

Father, I'm down in the dumps today. You are my unending
source of strength. Gather me in Your arms for always. Amen.

Today, God Wants You to Know...
He Sees What the World Doesn't

"Then your Father, who sees what is done in secret, will reward you."
MATTHEW 6:6 NIV

We live two lives. Our visible life is lived before others. Our secret life is lived solely before the Lord. Are they consistent? Many times the motive behind our actions is to impress others. Our real heart is revealed by what we do in secret, when only the Lord is watching.

How do we choose to spend our time and money? Do we pray aloud to look spiritual in the eyes of others? Are we generous to attain a certain reputation? Do we mention tithing and fasting to appear devout? When we look closely at our motives, we must admit that sometimes we are more concerned about gaining the applause of people than of God.

Perhaps your behind-the-scenes sacrifices are going unnoticed by the world. Do not be discouraged. God knows. He hears your prayers and sees what you are doing in secret to serve Him. Eternal treasures are being stored up in heaven. Your selfless acts will be rewarded. Do not give up and think it doesn't matter. It matters to God. Seek to please Him above anyone else. Live before an audience of One so that your life will honor Him.

Lord, help me walk consistently in Your truth. May what I do in secret bring glory to You. May I not seek others' approval, but Yours alone. Amen.

He Can Change Your Heart

I will take away their stony, stubborn heart and give them a tender,
responsive heart, so they will obey my decrees and regulations.
Then they will truly be my people, and I will be their God.
EZEKIEL 11:19–20 NLT

Rules—we live by them every day. We obey the rules of the road (don't drive too fast) and the rules created by our bosses (no personal work on company time). We abide by society's rules, too—we turn off our cell phones during movies and don't talk on elevators.

And as believers, we try to obey God's rules. We attempt to do God proud by not taking His name in vain and by going to church and giving money to ministries. We speak of Him when the opportunity arises, listen to godly music, and even wear Christian T-shirts!

But how much of our obedience is out of a sense of duty? After all, God wants us to obey Him *not* because we're afraid He'll punish us if we don't, but because we love Him. If you obey out of a sense of obligation, ask God to change your heart. Consider all He's done for you—given you His Son, forgiven your sins, answered your prayers. Remind yourself that He gave of Himself freely, with no strings attached.

When You meditate on His character and are convinced of His love for you, obedience will become not a duty but a delight.

Father, I praise You for the love that left heaven behind.
Help me to love You more.

Today, God Wants You to Know...
He Can Do Amazing Things through You

For we are labourers together with God:
ye are God's husbandry, ye are God's building.
1 CORINTHIANS 3:9 KJV

Isn't it amazing that God allows us to work with Him to accomplish great things for His kingdom? In reality God could have called on His angels to do the jobs He assigns to us. He could have chosen a method to fulfill His work that would have required less dealing with stubbornness and excuses; but God chose to use us—His human creation. What a wonderful privilege we have!

Not only does God choose to use us in His work; He also continues to work in our lives to mold us into the masterpieces He has planned. The more we allow Him to do *in* us, the more He will be able to do *through* us.

It is important to realize that God wants to work in and through us all our lives. We are not complete until we reach heaven, when we will see Christ as He is. If we become satisfied with who we are while yet on earth, it is pride—the beginning of our downfall. The more content we are with our spiritual maturity, the less God can use us. We must strive daily to be more like Christ if we desire to be useful to God.

Oh great God, it is an honor to serve You. I ask You to
work in my life that I might be useful to Your work.

Today, God Wants You to Know. . .
His Strength Is Your Strength

A final word: Be strong in the Lord and in his mighty power.
EPHESIANS 6:10 NLT

Have you ever thought about how strong God is? With the strength of His Word, He spoke the planets and stars into existence. That same strength pushed back the Red Sea so the Israelites could cross over. It was His strength that gave David the courage to face Goliath. It was His strength that helped Joshua face his enemies at Jericho. His strength invigorated Naomi and Ruth, and it resides inside every believer who calls on the name of Jesus.

How wonderful to realize we have such power at work within us. The very God of the universe strengthens us with His might, not ours. If it were up to us, we'd make a mess of things, wouldn't we? Oh, we might muster up a little strength on good days, but what about the bad ones?

Perhaps you've never fully understood what it means to tap into God's strength. Maybe you still don't feel strong. Begin to memorize scriptures like the one above. Put notes on your mirror, your refrigerator, and your bedside table as a reminder. Then begin to quote those scriptures on a daily basis and watch His strength within you begin to grow!

Lord, in myself I'm weak. I'm totally dependent on You.
Thank You that the same strength that resided in David, Joshua,
Naomi, and Ruth lives in me. In Your mighty power I am strong!

Today, God Wants You to Know...
He Measures His Wealth in Souls

"This is how much God loved the world: He gave his Son, his one and only Son. And this is why: so that no one need be destroyed; by believing in him, anyone can have a whole and lasting life."
JOHN 3:16 MSG

Productivity carries a lot of weight in business these days. It often weighs heavily in performance reviews that determine promotions and salary increases. With that in mind, it can sometimes seem difficult to balance productivity with the relationships we have with other people—especially those we work with each day.

We can become so wrapped up in the task we are trying to achieve that we forget that life is about the people—the relationships—God has put around us. We must be cautious not to be so focused on a task that we discount the value of others. We must disconnect from the task and focus on the person, and sometimes that means letting go of the work for a minute or two—long enough to really listen to what someone is saying. We need each other—as friends, family, or just passing acquaintances—in order to live successful lives.

God measures His wealth in souls. That should be our focus, too.

Lord, help me to know when it's time to drop the task and run to the relationship. Amen.

Today, God Wants You to Know . . .
His Goodness, Each and Every Day

I would have lost heart, unless I had believed that I would
see the goodness of the LORD in the land of the living.
PSALM 27:13 NKJV

While it's true that God has planned for us a life of joy in eternity with Him in heaven, He also has excellent plans for us here and now. God wants us to enjoy His goodness each day of our lives.

You can compare your earthly life to going on a cruise vacation or a road trip with your best friends. When you go on a trip, it shouldn't only be fun when you've reached a particular destination, but you should be enjoying yourself all along the journey. You plan to enjoy spending time with your friends as you participate in the activities provided on the ship or as you stop to see the sights that you pass as you drive. You expect to enjoy yourself along the way.

In the same way, God's goodness isn't just for when we get to heaven. God wants us to enjoy ourselves and Him all along the journey. Remember that He cares about your job, your family, your emotions, and the things that you care about. Look for the good that He is doing in your life and find joy in knowing that your Friend on the journey deeply cares for you.

Dear Lord, thank You for allowing me to see Your goodness each day.
Help me to enjoy the life You have given me. Amen.

Your Name Is Music to His Ears

But now, this is what the LORD says—he who created you, Jacob,
he who formed you, Israel: "Dear not fear, for I have redeemed you;
I have summoned you by name; you are mine."
ISAIAH 43:1 NIV

Do you remember the first day of school? The teacher called the roll, and you waited for your name to be announced. When it was, you knew that you were a part of that class—you belonged there.

We wait for our names to be called a lot in life: when captains pick teams, while sitting in a doctor's waiting room, or while waiting to be called in for a job interview. There is comfort in hearing our own names, in being recognized.

God knows your name. He created you and redeemed you from sin through His Son, Jesus, if you have accepted Him as your personal Savior. He knows you. He put together your personality and topped off His masterpiece by giving you all sorts of likes and dislikes, dreams and desires, passions and preferences. You are His unique design, His daughter, His beloved one.

No matter if you feel you don't belong, *you belong to God.* He takes great joy in you. You are His treasure. He sent Jesus to die on the cross to give you an abundant life. He wants to spend eternity with you! He calls you by name, and your name is music to your Father's ears.

Lord, I thank You for knowing my name
and loving me unconditionally. Amen.

Today, God Wants You to Know...
and Model the Fullness of His Grace

"Why do you look at the speck of sawdust in your brother's eye and pay no attention to the plank in your own eye?"

LUKE 6:41 NIV

Whether we admit it or not, we judge others. Maybe it's how they look ("Just how many tattoos does a person need?") or their political leaning ("How can you call yourself a Christian and vote for a president from *that* party?"). Sometimes we pigeonhole others because of an accent ("What an ignorant hillbilly!") or an achievement of some kind ("Mr. Smarty-Pants thinks he's better than everyone else because of his PhD.")

Our Father God urges us not to judge others in this way. After all, He doesn't look at our outward appearance. He doesn't pay attention to our political affiliation or anything else in our lives that is open to interpretation. He looks at the heart and judges us by whether we have a personal relationship with Him.

In Luke 6:41 Jesus reminds us through His sawdust/plank analogy that none of us are blameless. It's important to put our own shortcomings into perspective when we face the temptation to judge others. Today, work on removing the plank from your eye and praise God for His gift of grace!

God, please forgive me for the times that I have judged others. Help me to develop a gentle spirit that can share Your love and hope in a nonjudgmental way. Amen.

Today, God Wants You to Know . . .
He Will Help You Store Up Treasures in Heaven

"But store up for yourselves treasures in heaven, where neither
moth nor rust destroys, and where thieves do not break in or steal;
for where your treasure is, there your heart will be also."
MATTHEW 6:20–21 NASB

Treasure maps show up regularly in children's stories and pirate movies. What is so intriguing about a treasure map? It leads to treasure! People have gone to great lengths in search of treasure, sometimes only to find in the end that the map was a hoax and no treasure existed.

Imagine a treasure map drawn of your life, with all its twists and turns. Where do you spend your time? How do you use your talents? Would the map lead to heaven, or is your treasure in earthly things?

Each day consists of twenty-four hours, regardless of how we use them. We make choices about the priorities in our lives. The world sends messages about how we should spend our time; however, if we listen to the still, small voice of God, we will learn how to "store up treasures in heaven."

Nurturing relationships and sharing Christ with others, as well as reading God's Word and getting to know Him through prayer, are examples of storing up treasures in heaven. Using our gifts for His glory is also important. The dividends of such investments are priceless.

Eternal God, help me to store up treasures in heaven with the
choices I make today. Give me opportunities to show Your love.
Remind me of the importance of time spent with You. Amen.

His Presence Brings Blessings

"Come, follow me," Jesus said, "and I will send you out to fish for people."
MATTHEW 4:19 NIV

The beach was empty except for one lone walker near the water's edge. With every step she took, her feet left an impression in the sand. But as the waves lapped upon the shore, her footprints quickly vanished. Following her footsteps would have been impossible unless someone were walking close behind.

Jesus asked His disciples to follow Him, and He asks us to do the same. It sounds simple, but following Jesus can be a challenge. Sometimes we become impatient, not wanting to wait upon the Lord. We run ahead of Him by taking matters into our own hands and making decisions without consulting Him first. Or perhaps we aren't diligent to keep in step with Him. We fall behind, and soon Jesus seems so far away.

Following Jesus requires staying right on His heels. We need to be close enough to hear His whisper. Stay close to His heart by opening the Bible daily. Allow His Word to speak to your heart and give you direction. Throughout the day, offer up prayers for guidance and wisdom. Keep in step with Him, and His close presence will bless you beyond measure.

Dear Lord, grant me the desire to follow You.
Help me not to run ahead or to lag behind. Amen.

He Will Give You the Desires of Your Heart

Delight thyself also in the LORD:
and he shall give thee the desires of thine heart.
PSALM 37:4 KJV

What is it that you most desire? Is it a successful career or large bank account? Do you wish for someone with whom you can share romantic dinners or scenic bike rides? It really doesn't matter. What does matter is that you are fully committed to God. When that is the case, the desires in your heart will be the ones He places there. He will grant them because they honor Him.

Too many times we look at God's promises as some sort of magic formula. We fail to realize that His promises have more to do with our own relationship with Him. It begins with a heart's desire to live your life in a way that pleases God. Only then will fulfillment of His promises take place.

The promise in Psalm 37:4 isn't intended for personal gain—although that is sometimes a side benefit. It is meant to glorify God. God wants to give you the desires of your heart when they line up with His perfect plan. As you delight in Him, His desires will become your desires, and you will be greatly blessed.

Lord, I know You want to give me the desires of my heart.
Help me live in a way that makes this possible.

Today, God Wants You to Know. . .
It's Time to Give

"Give, and it will be given to you. A good measure, pressed down,
shaken together and running over, will be poured into your lap.
For with the measure you use, it will be measured to you."
LUKE 6:38 NIV

Every day you encounter opportunities to serve others. You may have a sick friend who needs help cleaning her house. An elderly person at your church may need assistance with her shopping. A coworker could use some help meeting a deadline. The list of possibilities is endless.

The Bible tells us to help carry each other's loads. You may think you have nothing to give, but as a child of God, your supply is greater than you imagine. You can serve others by giving your time, a kind word, a listening ear, financial aid, or even physical work. Give, not because you have to, but because you want to. God appreciates a gift given with a servant's heart.

There's someone out there who needs your help. Ask God to show you that person and what you can do to help meet their needs. Giving to others will always bring an abundance of blessings back to you. So what are you waiting for? It's time to give!

Dear God, help me to give to others in a way that
will bring glory and honor to Your name. Amen.

Troubles Are Only Temporary

Fig trees may no longer bloom, or vineyards produce grapes;
olive trees may be fruitless, and harvest time a failure;
sheep pens may be empty, and cattle stalls vacant—
*but I will still celebrate because the L*ORD *God saves me.*

HABAKKUK 3:17–18 CEV

Have you ever had a day when everything has gone wrong? The neighbor's dogs bark all night, so you don't get any sleep. You spill coffee on your favorite blouse. The car has a flat tire. You're running late, so you get a ticket for speeding. You end up wondering what next—what else can go wrong?

On days like this it's hard to find any reason to be joyful. How can we be happy when every time we turn around another disaster strikes? Instead of greeting everyone with a smile, on these down days we tend to be cranky or snarly. We tell anyone willing to listen about our terrible lot in life.

Rejoicing in the Lord is not a matter of circumstances but of will. We can choose to remember the God of our salvation and be content with His love for us. No matter how much goes awry, we have so much more to be thankful for because of the grace of God.

God is sovereign. With His help we can rise above the worry of our circumstances to find peace and contentment. Then, no matter what is happening in our lives, other people will see the joy of God.

Thank You, God, that You have provided for my salvation and my joy.
Help me to look to You instead of dwelling on my momentary troubles.
Amen.

He Is Your Encourager

So we say with confidence, "The Lord is my helper;
I will not be afraid. What can mere mortals do to me?"
HEBREWS 13:6 NIV

Remember when you were a kid and you had a school project due? The whole thing seemed overwhelming until your father said, "Let me help you with that." He listened to your ideas then helped you make the necessary purchases. Finally, the day arrived to put together your project. Instead of doing the work for you, your father simply made his presence known as you worked—encouraging you with, "That's great, honey!" and "Wow, I can hardly wait to see this when it's done!" His words boosted your confidence and spurred you on.

Your heavenly Father is a "That's great, honey" kind of encourager. Talk about building your confidence! When you're up against a tough situation He's standing right there, speaking positive words over you, telling you you've got what it takes to be the best you can possibly be. And while He won't take the reins—He wants you to learn from the experience, after all—He will advise you as you go.

What are you facing today? Do you need a helper? God is the very best. Just knowing He's there will ease your mind and invigorate you for the tasks you face.

Father, I'm so glad You stand nearby, whispering words of
encouragement. You're the best helper possible. Thank You for
taking my fears and replacing them with godly confidence.

He Will Care for You

"Consider how the wild flowers grow. They do not labor or spin. Yet I tell
you, not even Solomon in all his splendor was dressed like one of these.
If that is how God clothes the grass of the field, which is here today,
and tomorrow is thrown into the fire, how much more
will he clothe you—you of little faith!"
LUKE 12:27–28 NIV

Take a look at God's creation. He has created this world with
such intricate detail. He designed every tree, the majestic
mountains, a glorious sun, and a mysterious moon. Each animal
has been given unique markings, parts, and sounds. Consider the
long-necked giraffe, the massive elephant, the graceful swan, and
the perfectly striped zebra!

If God makes the flowers, each type unique and beautiful, and
if He sends the rain and sun to meet their needs, will He not care
for you as well?

He made you. What the Father makes, He loves. And that
which He loves, He cares for. We were made in His image. Humans are dearer to God than any of His other creations. Rest in
Him. Trust Him. Just as He cares for the birds of the air and the
flowers of the meadows, God is in the business of taking care of
His sons and daughters. Let Him take care of you.

Father, I am amazed by Your creation. Remind me that I am Your
treasured child. Take care of me today as only You can do. Amen.

He Will Give You a Fresh Perspective

*But do not forget this one thing, dear friends: With the Lord a day is
like a thousand years, and a thousand years are like a day.*

2 PETER 3:8 NIV

Imagine that your workday was five minutes long. You'd hardly
have time to clock in and get settled at your desk. You'd maybe
have a minute or two to check e-mail, and suddenly the day would
be over. The time would fly.

But what if you spent five minutes sitting at a stoplight? It
would seem like an eternity. Five minutes can fly by, or it can drag
on forever. It all depends on your perspective.

For Jonah, spending a few nights in the belly of a fish changed
his perspective from doing whatever he could to avoid God to
doing whatever he could to follow Him obediently. For Job, losing
everything changed his perspective from enjoying life's luxuries
to falling on his knees and begging God to deliver him. For Saul,
a blinding light changed his perspective from investing his life in
hunting down Christians and persecuting them to pouring out his
life at the foot of the cross.

If you are feeling worried, burdened, or overwhelmed, take a
step back and look at the big picture. Ask God to give you some
of His perspective. Maintaining a biblical perspective on our
circumstances can mean the difference between peace and anxiety,
between sorrow and joy.

*Father, I admit that I often become discouraged by
my circumstances. Please give me a fresh perspective
and help me to see my life through Your eyes. Amen.*

Today, God Wants You to Know...
His Creation Is for Your Enjoyment

When I consider your heavens, the work of your fingers,
the moon and the stars, which you have set in place, what is
mankind that you are mindful of them. . .[and] care for them?
PSALM 8:3–4 NIV

When we reflect on the world around us—the beauty of trees, mountains, streams—it staggers the imagination. Looking up into the heavens, gazing at planets and stars light-years away, we are humbled. Just think: God, in His infinite wisdom, has created all these things with His mighty hands, just as He created us.

Viewing and considering such magnificence puts everything into perspective. Our problems seem miniscule in comparison to the heavens above, the majesty of the mountains, and the grandeur of the trees. Knowing that God has favored us with His grace, mercy, and love, and has given us the responsibility to care for those things He has put into our hands, fills us with songs of praise.

If life is getting you down, if your problems seem insurmountable, take a walk. Look around, below, and above you. Take a deep breath. Draw close to a tree and touch its bark, examine its leaves. Look down at the spiders, ants, and grass. Feel the wonder of the earth. Thank Him for the heavens—the sun, moon, and stars—above you. This is what God has created for us, for you. Praise His worthy name.

Lord, the beauty of this earth is so awesome. In the glory of
all You have created, thank You for caring so much about me,
for creating the magnificence that surrounds me, and for
giving up Your Son, Jesus, for all our sakes. Amen.

Today, God Wants You to Know...
You Are Uniquely Made

You made all the delicate, inner parts of my body
and knit me together in my mother's womb.
PSALM 139:13 NLT

At the moment of your conception, roughly three million decisions were made about you. Everything from your eye color and the number of your wisdom teeth, to the shape of your nose and the swirl of your fingerprints, was determined in the blink of an eye.

Now consider that there are approximately six billion human beings alive on this planet today, and each of *them* was as individually crafted as you. If that thought isn't staggering enough, think about this: it's estimated that as many as 100 billion people have walked the earth at one time or another—and each of *them* was uniquely made. Wow. How can we even begin to fathom the God who is responsible for all that?

He is a big God. Unfathomable. Incomparable. Frankly, words just don't do Him justice. And He made *you*. You were knit together by a one-of-a-kind, amazing God who is absolutely, undeniably, head-over-heels, crazy in love with you. Try to wrap your brain around that!

Heavenly Father and Creator, thank You for the
amazing gift of life, for my uniqueness and individuality.
Help me to use my life as a gift of praise to You. Amen.

Your Pure Motives Bring Glory to Him

Every man's work shall be made manifest: for the
day shall declare it, because it shall be revealed by fire;
and the fire shall try every man's work of what sort it is.
1 CORINTHIANS 3:13 KJV

Churches offer many places for God's children to serve. There are areas in children's ministries—nurseries, classrooms, music programs, or vacation Bible school—that are often strapped for willing workers. Maybe volunteering to clean the building or help with upkeep is more your style. Does your church have a nursing home ministry or food pantry ministry? Are you involved?

Do you genuinely wish to help in some of these areas to bring glory to God? If you get involved, you will be blessed beyond measure. We are all called to be useful for Christ. When we do so willingly and with a servant's heart, the joy that fills us will be indescribable and lasting.

On the other hand, if our service is merely to receive praise and recognition from our peers, we'll receive our reward, but it won't be the blessing of God that it could have been. God knows our hearts. He recognizes our motives and rewards us accordingly.

Lord, I want to serve You with a pure heart.
Let all I do bring glory to You.

Today, God Wants You to Know...
You Can!

I can do all things through Christ who strengthens me.
PHILIPPIANS 4:13 NKJV

If you've been walking with the Lord for any length of time, you've probably quoted Philippians 4:13. Maybe you even memorized it during a rough season as a reminder. We know—in our heads, anyway—that we can do anything through Christ Jesus who strengthens us. But knowing this and believing it are two separate things.

Do you really believe you can do all things through Christ Jesus? All things? If not, then it's likely you're still relying on your own strength to get things done. It's human nature to try to handle things on our own, after all. But the same God who created the heavens and the earth stands ready to work through you. Talk about power! It's above and beyond anything we could ever ask or think.

If you're struggling to believe God can and will work through you to accomplish great things, spend some time in prayer today. Acknowledge that you've been trying to do things on your own. Change your "I can't" attitude to "I can!" Then prepare yourself to be infused with strength from on high. Fully submit yourself to the One who longs to do great things—both in you and through you!

Lord, I'll be the first to admit I try to do things on my own.
I often leave You out of the equation. Today I lean on Your strength.
Remind me daily that I can do all things through You.

No Matter What Happens,
He Will Keep You Safe

Take the sword of the Spirit, which is the word of God.
EPHESIANS 6:17 NLT

An anchor is usually made out of metal and is used to hold a ship to the bottom of a body of water. It is interesting to note that wind and currents are not the largest forces an anchor has to overcome, but the vertical movement of waves.

God gave us the Bible to serve us much as an anchor serves a boat. The Bible is filled with valuable information for your mission on earth. God's Word can set your mind at peace and hold you steady through life's storms. The truth found within its pages is your assurance that no matter what you face in this battle of life, God will bring you safely home.

Take a new approach to God's Word. Let it breathe new revelation—new life—into your heart. Expect knowledge and understanding of God's Word to become personal, as if it were written just for you. Anchor your soul by believing what you read, and know that the promises of God assure that the victory belongs to you.

God, I know the Bible is true and full of wisdom for my life.
Help me to grow and to understand what I read and apply it to my life.
Amen.

Today, God Wants You to Know...
He Is Your Sanctuary

O God, You are my God; early will I seek You; my soul thirsts for You; my flesh longs for You in a dry and thirsty land where there is no water. So I have looked for You in the sanctuary, to see Your power and Your glory.
PSALM 63:1–2 NKJV

The word *sanctuary* may make you think of a church, an altar, a place of quiet beauty, a place to worship. You may also think of a place of rest and safety where animals may live protected. At various times in history, a sanctuary was a place of refuge where even accused criminals could seek shelter.

Christ Himself is our sanctuary. The psalmist speaks of hungering and thirsting, both body and soul. What is he looking for? He is searching for God. Clearly he did not find salvation in the dry, thirsty land where there was no water, and neither will we. The world's offerings, its counsel, and its substances have nothing to sustain us. Satisfaction can be found only in relationship with Jesus Christ, the One who called Himself living water and bread of life. The power and glory of God are manifest in Him. In Matthew 11:28 Jesus tells us to come to Him and we will find rest for our souls. Christ Himself is the sanctuary, the place of rest, protection, and shelter.

Lord Jesus, forgive me for seeking rest and satisfaction in the desert of this world. Thank You for being my sanctuary.

Today, God Wants You to Know...
You Are a Letter from Him

*You are a letter from Christ. . . This "letter" is written
not with pen and ink, but with the Spirit of the living God.
It is carved not on tablets of stone, but on human hearts.*
2 CORINTHIANS 3:3 NLT

Most of us can't go a day or even a few hours without checking our e-mail. It's fast, it's free, and it's practical. But don't you just love it when you go to the mailbox, and stuck between a bunch of bills is a letter from a good friend or loved one? Doesn't that just make your day? A real letter is special because you know the other person took the time to think about you and went to the trouble to purchase a stamp and handwrite a precious note just for you. That beats an e-mail any day!

We've all heard it said that sometimes we are the only Bible a person will ever read. We are a letter from Christ. When you are sharing your faith, or even in your everyday relationships, always try to go the extra mile with people. Go beyond "fast, free, and practical." Be more than an e-mail: be a precious letter from Christ and take the time to let them know how loved and treasured they are by you and by the Lord!

*Father, help me to make the people in my life feel
loved and cherished. Help me to remember that I
am a letter from You as I interact with others. Amen.*

You Can Give Your Problems to Him

Be angry, and do not sin. Meditate within
your heart on your bed, and be still.

PSALM 4:4 NKJV

When we are swept up in a flurry of anger, words sometimes fly from our mouths in a tone that injures others. Maybe we go so far as to slam doors, yell and scream, even throw things. Anger, at times, is inevitable; but does it have to be sinful and destructive?

The psalmist tells us to be still when we feel anger well up inside, to meditate on our beds when we're staring anger in the face. When we pause to meditate, to go to a quiet place to get alone with God and be still, we are choosing to let Him have control in the situation. We are acknowledging our weakness and giving Him the opportunity to display His strength in us. In going to God about our anger, we open the door for Him to calm us and to reveal to us the truth of the situation that angered us. In handing over our feelings of anger, we make room for peace.

What situations in your life cause anger to flare up in your heart? Before you're experiencing the heat of the moment, give these problems over to God. He'll prepare your heart to deal with each situation the way He wants you to.

Lord, enable me to trust You wholly
with my anger and keep me from sin.

He Will Take Care of the Small Stuff, Too

> *Daniel answered and said: "Blessed be the name of*
> *God forever and ever, for wisdom and might are His."*
> DANIEL 2:20 NKJV

When God brings us through a trial, do we worship Him with great thankfulness, or do we take that blessing as our due? Though God is great, He doesn't appreciate being taken for granted any more than we would.

Required to describe King Nebuchadnezzar's bad dream to him or face imminent death, Daniel didn't worry or have a pity party. Instead, he called a prayer meeting of his three best friends. In the middle of the night, God answered their prayers, revealing Nebuchadnezzar's dream to Daniel, the wisest of the Babylonian king's wise men.

Daniel's first and very grateful response, in the midst of his relief, was to praise the Lord who had saved his life. He gave God recognition for His saving grace even before he went to see the king who had threatened to kill him.

We may believe that our Lord answers in such life-and-death situations, but do we have confidence that He takes care of smaller troubles, too? And when He does respond to an ordinary situation, do we give thanks?

Make me thankful, Lord, for all the ways in which You bless and care for me. I don't want my life to become laden with ungratefulness. Amen.

Today, God Wants You to Know. . .
You Are His Greatest Creation

When I consider your heavens, the work of your fingers, the moon and the stars, which you have set in place, what is mankind that you are mindful of them, human beings that you care for them?
PSALM 8:3–4 NIV

Do you ever spend time thinking about the vastness of God? His greatness? His majesty? When you ponder His creation—the heavens, the moon, and the stars—do you feel tiny in comparison? Do you wonder how, in the midst of such greatness, He even remembers your name, let alone the details of your life or the problems you go through?

Daughter of God, you are important to your heavenly Father, more important than the sun, the moon, and the stars. You are created in the image of God, and He cares for you. In fact, He cares so much that He sent His Son, Jesus, to offer His life as a sacrifice for your sins.

The next time you look up at the heavens, the next time you ooh and aah over a majestic mountain or emerald waves crashing against the shoreline, remember that those things, in all of their splendor, don't even come close to you—God's greatest creation.

Oh Father, when I look at everything You have created, I'm so overwhelmed with who You are. Who am I that You would think twice about me? And yet You do. You love me, and for that I'm eternally grateful!

Today, God Wants You to Know. . .
He Is Your Good Shepherd

You've kept track of my every toss and turn through the sleepless nights,
each tear entered in your ledger, each ache written in your book.
PSALM 56:8 MSG

In heaven there will be no more sadness. Tears will be a thing of the past. For now, we live in a fallen world. There are heartaches and disappointments. Some of us are more prone to crying than others, but all of us have cause to weep at times.

Call out to God when you find yourself tossing and turning at night, or when tears drench your pillow. He is a God who sees, a God who knows. He is your *Abba* Father, your Daddy.

It hurts the Father's heart when you cry, but He sees the big picture. God knows that gut-wrenching trials create perseverance in His beloved daughter and that perseverance results in strong character.

Do you ever wonder if God has forgotten you and left you to fend for yourself? Rest assured that He has not left you even for one moment. He is your Good Shepherd, and you are His lamb. When you go astray, He spends every day and every night calling after you. If you are a believer, then you know your Good Shepherd's voice.

Shhhh. . .listen. . .He is whispering a message of comfort even now.

Father, remind me that You are a God who sees my pain. Jesus,
I thank You that You gave up Your life for me. Holy Spirit,
comfort me in my times of deep sadness. Amen.

He Will Be Your Hiding Place

You are my hiding place; you will protect me from
trouble and surround me with songs of deliverance.
PSALM 32:7 NIV

We all need a place to rest. Life is busy and stressful. Look around you and designate a place to rest. It may be in your bedroom, your living room, at a park, in your backyard, on a patio or deck, or even on a tiny apartment balcony.

When you have found the physical place of rest, then look to Jesus. He is your hiding place, a haven, a quietness, a hug from God Himself. Give the Lord your worries, your troubles, and your questions. Give Him your praise and thanksgiving, too. When your day has been especially long, when you feel alone and empty and hopeless, ask your Savior to sing over you. He promises to sing songs of deliverance over you.

Like a mother sings lullabies and rocks her baby to sleep, so your Redeemer longs to hide you from the pressures of this great big world and give you peaceful rest. Hold on to Jesus. All the days of your life He will be a hiding place for you.

Jesus, be my refuge, my place of rest. Sometimes I feel so
alone and so weary of trying, trying, trying. Lift my burdens.
Sing songs of deliverance over me, I ask. Amen.

You Were Made to Laugh

Our mouths were filled with laughter, our tongues with songs of joy.
PSALM 126:2 NIV

Comedians live their lives to make people laugh. From famous actors on the movie screen to the class clown at a local high school, we take a moment to celebrate with them. Sometimes the many worries in life keep us from letting our guard down, relaxing, and enjoying the little things in life that bring us great joy and laughter.

It feels good to laugh—from a small giggle that you keep to yourself to a great big belly laugh. It is a wonderful stress reliever or tension breaker. How many times have you been in an awkward situation or in a stressful position and laughter erupted? It breaks the tension and sets our hearts and minds at ease.

As children of the Creator Himself, we were made to laugh—to experience great joy. Our design didn't include for us to carry stress, worry, and heaviness every day. When was the last time you really had a good laugh? Have you laughed so hard that tears rolled down your cheeks? Go ahead! Have a good time! Ask God to give you a really good laugh today.

> *Lord, help me rediscover laughter. Help me to take every*
> *opportunity You provide to see the joy in life and the*
> *comedy that it brings to my world every day. Amen.*

Today, God Wants You to Know. . .

He Will Meet You in the Wee Hours of the Night

I will praise the LORD, who counsels me;
even at night my heart instructs me.
PSALM 16:7 NIV

For us women, the nighttime hours are often difficult. When the chaos of the day settles down and our head hits the pillow, we're free to think. . .about everything. Problems. Relationship issues. Job concerns. Decisions. The "what ifs." The "I should haves." Sometimes our thoughts wander for hours. We toss and turn, and sleep won't come.

If you're like this, if you find nighttime difficult, then it's time for a change of thinking. Instead of looking at the night as problematic, look at it as your one-on-one time with the Lord. He longs to meet you in the wee hours of the night. He wants to chase away any unnecessary worries and give you everything you need to sleep like a baby.

How encouraging to know that God longs to counsel us—to advise. And He's fully aware that nighttime is hard. So instead of fretting when you climb into bed, spend that time with Him. Use the nighttime as your special time with God. Meet with Him and expect to receive His counsel.

Lord, nighttimes are hard sometimes. I want to trust You. I want to put my head on the pillow and fall fast asleep. But the cares of the day overwhelm me. Father, I trust Your counsel. Speak to me in the night. Instruct my heart.

His Focus Is on Your Journey

"Worship and serve him with your whole heart and a willing mind.
For the LORD sees every heart and knows every plan and thought.
If you seek him, you will find him."

1 CHRONICLES 28:9 NLT

God's view of success is vastly different from the world's. God asks that we give ourselves to Him in worship. We find our success in earnestly seeking after God and following His commands.

On the other hand, the world says that we must have a good job, make lots of money, buy the newest toys, and focus on making ourselves happy. The world doesn't care how we accomplish these things. If we have to be superficial, fine. If we have to tell a lie here or there, no problem. If we have to pretend to be something we are not, who cares?

God cares. God sees our hearts and knows our motives—good or bad. The world's mind-set looks to the tangible elements of success. A good car, a nice job, and a big house indicate success, regardless of how we obtained them. On the other hand, God's focus is on our journey. We may not live in the biggest house on the block, and we may not even own a car, but those things are not important to God. Instead, worshipping and serving God with our whole hearts, being genuine and sincere, and willingly seeking God are the indicators of true success in God's eyes.

Dear Lord, teach me to seek after You willingly,
with sincere motives. Please help me focus on pleasing
You rather than seeking success by worldly standards. Amen.

Today, God Wants You to Know...
He Will Show You the Way

The highway of the upright is to depart from evil;
he who keeps his way preserves his soul.
PROVERBS 16:17 NKJV

Type a few words and click your mouse a couple of times and you can find directions to anywhere in the world. With minimal effort, you can have step-by-step instructions, maps, and even satellite images of the places you want to go and the best route to get there. All you need is a starting point and a final destination.

Life is a journey, and we are traveling a highway to a final destination. There is a road that will take us where we want to go, but there are also many opportunities to take detours—sin that distracts us from the path God has laid for us.

But there is direction to be found! In solitude, reflection, and self-examination we often hear God speak. In these times of prayer, He will show us the wrong turns we have taken and give us the opportunity to turn back to Him. He will set us back on the right path.

Ask God what He wants for you. What is the destination for your heart? Are you staying on the right road? Do you need to set some boundaries for yourself so you can better hear His voice? He is ready to show you the way.

Father, help me to be still, to sit in silence and listen for Your voice.
Show me the boundaries I need for my life and give me
grace to repent when I have strayed.

Today, God Wants You to Know...
He Will Meet You Wherever You Are

Adam and his wife hid themselves from the presence of the
Lord God amongst the trees of the garden. And the Lord God
called unto Adam, and said unto him, Where art thou?
Genesis 3:8–9 kjv

Throughout the Bible, God asks us questions, inviting us to dialogue with Him. The very first question God asked called Adam and Eve to self-awareness. *"Where are you?"* Of course God knew where the couple was that night. He asked to make them aware of where they were.

God waits for us at the appointed hour. He hovers over the latest Bible study guide and the beautifully illustrated prayer journal. He longs to listen to the words that pour out from our hearts. He remains eager to speak to us through His written Word and the Holy Spirit. But too many pages of the journal remain blank, and the Bible bookmark doesn't change places.

Today God still whispers, *"Where are you?"* God wants to spend time with us, but too often we hide among the trees of our gardens, the routines of everyday life. We have e-mails to answer, car repairs to see to, clothes to wash, phone calls to answer—and another appointment with God gets broken. The more appointments we break, the easier it becomes to forget.

Take a moment to answer God's question. He will meet you wherever you are.

Dear heavenly Father, teach me the discipline of spending time
with You. Let me listen and answer when You call. Amen.

Today, God Wants You to Know...
He Longs to Spend Time with You

I observed everything going on under the sun, and really,
it is all meaningless—like chasing the wind.
ECCLESIASTES 1:14 NLT

All Ashley really wanted was some quiet time sitting outside on her porch swing to read her devotions. Just as she sat down, her cell phone beeped, indicating that she needed to check her voice mail. As she listened to her messages, she heard reminders about meetings at work, a vet appointment for her cat, a bridal shower for a close friend, an invitation to a home cookware party, and a request for her to volunteer in the church nursery. It was enough to make her heart pound in her chest. She immediately forgot about her reading and began the task of scheduling all of those events on her calendar.

There will always be things that need to be done. There will always be people who want our time. We can become wind-chasers and focus on all of the things that this world is calling us to do. But Christ Jesus wants our time, too. He doesn't want us to feel overburdened or stressed. Ask God to help you see what things in your life are necessary and important as you let Him help you focus on the best things that He desires for you.

Dear God, help me to prioritize the tasks in my life and be able to say no
to the activities that take away from what You have planned for me.

Your Body Was Created to Worship Him

*Therefore, I urge you, brothers and sisters, in view of God's mercy,
to offer your bodies as a living sacrifice, holy and
pleasing to God—this is your true and proper worship.*

ROMANS 12:1 NIV

Mirror, mirror, on the wall, who's the fairest of them all? Full lips. Wrinkle-free faces. Size 4 bodies. Our culture worships the physically attractive. God created our bodies. What should our attitude be toward them? Do we adopt the world's view or God's design?

Society worships the body and neglects the spirit. We may be equally guilty of spending much time, money, and energy trying to perfect our bodies. People look at the outward appearance, but God looks at the heart. What are we doing to assure that our hearts are acceptable to Him? God created the body as a temple for our spirit. Like an oyster protecting a pearl, so our bodies are merely physical shells, protecting the real jewel, our eternal souls.

God created our bodies so that we could worship Him in spirit. As we offer our bodies as living sacrifices, we are worshipping our Creator. Sacrifice means putting aside our own needs for the sake of another. Our physical bodies are de-emphasized so our spiritual worth can take precedence. May the Lord teach us to put our bodies in proper perspective so they may be used for God's glory, not solely for others' appreciation.

*Dear Lord, help me to desire to offer my
body to You in spiritual worship. Amen.*

Today, God Wants You to Know...
He Is All You Need

*Whom have I in heaven but you? And earth has nothing
I desire besides you. My flesh and my heart may fail,
but God is the strength of my heart and my portion forever.*
PSALM 73:25–26 NIV

Do you ever feel like you have a weak heart? Feel like you're not strong? You crater at every little thing? Do you face life's challenges with your emotions in turmoil instead of facing them head-on with courage and strength? If so, you're not alone. Twenty-first-century women are told they can "be it all" and "do it all," but it's not true. God never meant for us to be strong every moment of our lives. If we were, we wouldn't need Him.

Here's the good news: you don't have to be strong. In your weakness, God's strength shines through. And His strength surpasses anything you could produce, even on your best day. It's the same strength that spoke the heavens and the earth into existence. The same strength that parted the Red Sea. And it's the same strength that made the journey up the hill to the cross.

So how do you tap into that strength? There's really only one way. Come into His presence. Spend some quiet time with Him. Acknowledge your weakness; then allow His strong arms to encompass you. There's really nothing else in heaven or on earth to compare. God is all you will ever need.

*Father, I feel so weak at times. It's hard just to put one
foot in front of the other. But I know You are my strength.
Invigorate me with that strength today, Lord.*

Today, God Wants You to Know...

Your Spiritual Muscles Need a Workout

Do not be wise in your own eyes; fear the LORD and shun evil.
This will bring health to your body and nourishment to your bones.
PROVERBS 3:7–8 NIV

Feeling run down? Has your spiritual fervor left? Do you need a boost in your body and spirit?

Obeying and living by God's principles produces life and health. Just as we exercise to strengthen our bodies, we must use our spiritual muscles to attain the strength, peace, and prosperity we all need and desire.

An ancient proverb reads: "He who has health has hope; and he who has hope has everything." As we pray, read, and meditate on God's Word, we increase our spiritual stamina. Although our circumstances may not change, the Lord gives us a new perspective filled with the hope and assurance that we may have lacked before. Exercising our faith produces character and a stronger foundation of trust in the Lord.

Consider this: medicine left in the cabinet too long loses its potency; masking tape loses its adhesiveness with time; old paint hardens in the can. So when was the last time you shook out the old bones and got moving? A workout for the body and spirit may be just the medicine you need!

Dear Lord, please help me out of my spiritual and physical rut.
As I seek Your strength, revive my soul and touch my
body with Your healing power, I pray. Amen.

He's Got It Covered—*All* of It!

"Bless my family; keep your eye on them always.
You've already as much as said that you would, Master GOD!
Oh, may your blessing be on my family permanently!"

2 SAMUEL 7:29 MSG

God is completely trustworthy. Think about that for a moment. When we can't trust others, we can trust Him. When we can't trust ourselves, we can trust Him. God keeps an eye on everyone at all times. He's got things under control, especially when we loosen our grip.

Did you know that you can trust God with both your own life *and* the lives of your family members? And that includes every single person in your family. Parents, grandparents, siblings, children, aunts, uncles—everyone. You can trust the Lord with their dreams, their goals, their aspirations, their attitudes, their reactions, their problems. You can trust Him to handle any relationship problems. God's got it covered. All of it.

Today, recommit yourself to trusting God with your family. Don't fret and don't try to fix people. That's not your job, after all. And besides, God's keeping an eye on everyone. He's said it, and you can believe it. It's in His master plan to bless your family. . .permanently!

God, I confess I sometimes struggle where my family is concerned. I want
to fix people. I want to fix situations. Thank You for the reminder that
You have great plans, not just for me, but for my family members, too.

He Will Help You Through

> *By his divine power, God has given us*
> *everything we need for living a godly life.*
> 2 PETER 1:3 NLT

People need you—your family, your friends. Adding their needs to your commitments at school or work can sometimes be too much. Maybe your boss demands extra hours on a project or your sister needs you to help her with a family birthday party.

People pulling you here and there can have you going in circles. Somehow you keep pushing forward, not always sure where the strength comes from, but thankful in the end that you made it through the day.

In those situations you're stretching not just your physical body to the limit, but your mind and emotions as well. Stress can make you feel like a grape in a winepress. But there is good news. God has given you everything you need, but you must choose to use the wisdom He has provided. Don't be afraid to say no when you feel you just can't add one more thing to your to-do list. Limit your commitments, ask someone to take notes for you in a meeting you can't make, or carpool with someone who shares your child's extra-curricular activity.

Alleviate the pressure where you can and then know that His power will make up for the rest.

> *Lord, help me to do what I can do; and I'll trust*
> *You to do for me those things that I can't do. Amen.*

Today, God Wants You to Know...
Your Heart Defines You

They are not of the world, even as I am not of the world.
JOHN 17:16 NASB

The world sends women messages every day. You should be thin with long, flowing, gorgeous hair. You should be married to a man—tall, dark, and handsome, of course—and on your ring finger there should be a sparkling diamond. You should smell of the finest, most expensive perfume. And if you are to be loved, you should dress a certain way, talk a certain way, and live in a certain neighborhood.

But believers in Christ are not of this world. We are in it but not of it. We are visitors here, and heaven will be our eternal home. While we are here on earth, we must avoid believing the things the world whispers to us. It is okay if you are not beautiful in the world's eyes. God sees you as a beautiful daughter, important enough to give His Son's life for! Diamonds and perfume are not the definition of a woman. It is the heart that defines her, and if her heart is turned toward Jesus, it will shine brighter than any diamond ever could.

Father, remind me today to tune out the world as
I tune in to what You have to say about me. Amen.

Today, God Wants You to Know...
He Offered Himself Freely

The Spirit and the bride say, "Come!" And let the one who hears say,
"Come!" Let the one who is thirsty come; and let the one
who wishes take the free gift of the water of life.
REVELATION 22:17 NIV

Have you noticed lately that a lot of "free" things have many strings attached? Search the web, and you'll discover scores of ads that offer a supposedly free item *if* you'll do something. In our world, very few people really want to give anything away.

But Jesus gave His earthly life away without our asking Him to or paying Him beforehand. Love led Him to give all He could to draw some to Himself. Though He knew many would deny His gift, Jesus offered Himself freely.

The benefits are all on our side: new life and a relationship with our Creator. What can we offer the Omnipotent One? What could He require that we could fulfill for Him? Our Creator doesn't really need us. He simply chooses, out of His own generous nature, to give us new life.

As we drink deeply of the water of life, we recognize God's great gift. Grateful, we seek out ways to serve Him. But even if we gave all we had, we could never repay God. His gift would still be free.

Do you know people who could use the best, really free gift in the world? Tell them about Jesus!

Thank You, Lord, for giving me a really free gift—
the best anyone could offer. Amen.

Today, God Wants You to Know...

Prayer Changes Things

> *The king's heart is a stream of water in the*
> *hand of the LORD; he turns it wherever he will.*
> PROVERBS 21:1 ESV

Relationships can be difficult at times. Even when communication is good and both people are Christians, there is still conflict when two human beings have a long-term relationship with each other. Children, parents, coworkers, roommates, friends, sisters, former spouses, and in-laws can all frustrate us at one time or another. We have our own desires and goals we want to meet; they have their agendas and needs; and everyone has selfishness in his or her heart. How do we get beyond competing desires that conflict with each other and harm our relationships?

Prayer is a key ingredient in pursuing successful relationships. We can pray for our own hearts to change as well as the hearts of those we're in conflict with. God can and will shape our affections, and He can change the minds of those for whom we pray. It is not difficult for Him, yet we so easily forget to ask. What relationships in your life need prayer today?

Heavenly Father, there is nothing in my heart and mind
or in those of whom I love that You cannot change.
Turn my heart to You, to desire Your best for my life.

Today, God Wants You to Know...
Sometimes He Chooses to Remain Silent

> *GOD, are you avoiding me? Where are you when I need you?*
> PSALM 10:1 MSG

Do you ever feel like God is missing in action? Like He's hard to reach during the very times you need Him most? Have you ever wondered if the Lord is actually avoiding you during your times of crisis? If He even cares at all about what you're going through?

God isn't in the avoiding business. And He cares about you very much. In fact, He loves you deeply and is with you through thick and thin. If you're in a season in which His voice seems to be waning, take the time to listen more attentively. If you still can't hear His voice, remember there are times when He chooses to remain silent. That doesn't mean He's not there or that He doesn't care. Nothing could be further from the truth. Perhaps He's just waiting to see if you're going to act out of what you already know, what He's already taught you.

If God's voice isn't clear right now, think back to the last thing you heard Him speak to your heart. Act on that thing. Just keep walking in consistent faith, love, and hope. And before long, you'll be hearing His voice again. . .crystal clear.

> *Lord, I'm calling out to You today. Sometimes I feel like*
> *You're not there. Until I hear Your voice, I'm going to keep on*
> *believing, keep on hoping, and keep on living a life of faith.*

Today, God Wants You to Know...

You Can Find Security in Him

Therefore, there is now no condemnation
for those who are in Christ Jesus.
ROMANS 8:1 NIV

Every woman longs for security. But where can security be found—in a large investment portfolio, a job with benefits, or a loyal friend? Placing our trust in these things is like building our house on shifting sand. Investments tumble. Jobs end. Friends move. There are no guarantees. What is here today could easily be gone tomorrow. So is permanent security just an illusion?

Jesus Christ is the same yesterday, today, and forever. He is the Rock, not shifting sand. He is immutable—unchanging. Christ died for us while we were yet sinners. By accepting His gift of eternal life, we will never be condemned. Our security is rooted in Christ's unconditional love for us. It is not based upon our performance but upon who He is. There is nothing that can separate us from that love, including our poor choices or disobedience. Nothing can pluck us from His hand. He is ours and we are His. He has prepared a home in heaven for us and has given us the indwelling Holy Spirit as a deposit guaranteeing that promise.

That is the hope and assurance that we can stake our lives on. Embrace the eternal security that is yours in Christ Jesus!

Dear Lord, my security comes in knowing You.
Thank You for Your enduring love! Amen.

Today, God Wants You to Know...
True Understanding Comes through Hearing and Obeying

The fear of the LORD is the beginning of wisdom; all who follow his precepts have good understanding. To him belongs eternal praise.
PSALM 111:10 NIV

Living in the information age, we are easily duped into thinking that knowledge is the answer to all our problems. If we educate ourselves well on a given subject, we believe we can master it. If we identify all facets of a problem, we can solve it. But the truth is, knowing doesn't necessarily lead to doing. If it did, we would all be eating healthy foods and exercising regularly. Knowledge and obedience are not synonymous. Somewhere between the two is our will.

Scripture teaches us fearing the Lord—not gaining information—is the source of wisdom. It is in hearing and obeying, James 1:22 tells us, that we gain clear understanding. To be a hearer of the Word only is to be deceived. To be a doer of the Word removes the spiritual blind spots and keeps our vision clear. This is the difficult part, for doing the Word often involves repentance or giving up our own agendas. Fearing the Lord is living in reverent submission to Him, seeking His will and way in our lives. That is the starting point for a life of wisdom and understanding.

Lord, help me not to be deceived by trusting in knowledge alone. Show me the areas where I have heard and not done, and help me to obey. Give me a reverent fear of You.

Today, God Wants You to Know...
You Can Change the World

"This is my command—be strong and courageous! Do not be afraid or
discouraged. For the Lord your God is with you wherever you go."
JOSHUA 1:9 NLT

In the Word of God, women from all professions and back-
grounds are changed by grace and then, with the Holy Spirit's
help, transform the people around them. In the Old Testament,
God shines the light on a beauty queen (Esther) who saves an entire generation of people with her bravery. In Exodus, Moses' sister,
Miriam, exhorts her fellow Israelites to worship. And in the New
Testament, Lydia and Tabitha run successful businesses and invest
their profits in ministry to the poor.

God wants you to change your world, too. Does that thought
scare you? Whatever station God has called you to, He will equip
you for the task. Are you a businesswoman? He will guide you to
do your job with integrity and faithfulness. Do you have a class-
room of kids looking up to you? God will give you energy and
creativity to discipline, lead, and teach them. Perhaps you've felt
called to minister, and you wonder whether you've heard God right.
Through circumstances, scripture, and mature Christian mentors,
He will make clear the path He wants you to take.

Don't be afraid to follow God—wherever He leads. Women in
every era have changed the world because they remained faithful to
God and followed His leadership.

Lord, help me be strong and courageous as I follow You wherever
You lead. I want You to use me to help change the world.

Giving to Him Has Great Rewards

*Honor the LORD from your wealth and from the first of
all your produce; so your barns will be filled with plenty
and your vats will overflow with new wine.*

PROVERBS 3:9–10 NASB

Perhaps you think this verse doesn't apply to you because you
don't consider yourself wealthy. The only produce you have
comes from the grocery store. Barns and vats of wine may not be
your top priority. But this verse applies. Read these words: *Honor
the Lord. . .from the first of all.*

Our God is not a God of leftovers. He wants us to put Him
first. One way to honor God is to give Him our "firstfruits," the
best we have to offer. The truth is that everything we have comes
from God. The Bible calls us to cheerfully give back to the Lord
one-tenth of all we earn.

Giving to God has great reward. You may not have barns you
need God to fill, but you will reap the benefit in other ways. When
believers honor God by giving to Him, we can trust that He will
provide for our needs. In Malachi 3:10 we are challenged to test
God in our tithing. Start with your next paycheck. Make the check
that you dedicate to God's kingdom work the first one you write.
See if God is faithful to provide for you throughout the month.

*Lord, remind me not to separate my finances from my faith. All that I
have comes from Your hand. I will honor You with my firstfruits. Amen.*

Today, God Wants You to Know...
There Is Nothing He Cannot Do

My times are in your hands; deliver me from the
hands of my enemies, from those who pursue me.
PSALM 31:15 NIV

Our lives are composed of seconds, minutes, hours, days, weeks,
months, and years. We think in each of these increments in
different situations. Look at a clock and we think about seconds,
minutes, and hours. Our calendar shows us days, weeks, and
months. On a birthday or holiday, we reflect on a year. We may
think about the era in which we live and the culture around us that
inhabits that time frame. We may dwell too much in the past or
worry too much about our future. All of these are part of the times
that the psalmist places in God's hands.

Think about God's hands that hold our time. These are the
hands that fashioned the world. These are the hands that took a
rib from Adam and made Eve. These are the hands that healed
the blind and the lame. These are the hands that broke bread in an
upper room. These are the hands that were nailed to a cross. These
are the hands graciously extended to doubting Thomas. Our times,
from our moments to our years, are in the hands of the Creator,
Healer, Sustainer, Provider, Redeemer, and Lover of our souls.
There is nothing He cannot do. Knowing this, the psalmist releases
his fears to God—so can you.

Gracious God, who rules and reigns over all my days,
cause me to remember that I am held by Your loving hands.

Even When Miracles Don't Come, You Can Still Trust Him

God gave Paul the power to perform unusual miracles.
When handkerchiefs or aprons that had merely touched
his skin were placed on sick people, they were healed.
ACTS 19:11–12 NLT

It's probably safe to say none of your clothing has ever resulted in an amazing healing. Maybe we have witnessed some unexplainable cures. We prayed, and God healed a friend of cancer. Perhaps God spared a loved one in an accident that claimed the lives of others. Most of the time, however, these kinds of miracles don't happen.

When his fellow missionary, Trophimus, fell sick, Paul was given no miracle to help him. When Timothy complained of frequent stomach problems, Paul had no miracle-working handkerchief for Timothy's misery. Paul himself suffered from an incurable ailment (2 Corinthians 12:7), yet he was willing to leave it with God. We, too, may be clueless as to why God miraculously heals others, but not us or our best friend.

Like Paul, we must trust God when there's no miracle. Can we be as resilient as Job, who said, "Though he slay me, yet will I trust in him" (Job 13:15 KJV)? We can—waiting for the day when health problems and bad accidents and death cease forever (Revelation 21:4).

When healing doesn't come, Lord Jesus,
give us grace to trust You more. Amen.

Today, God Wants You to Know...
He Will Be There through All of Life's Changes

Jesus Christ is the same yesterday, today, and forever.
HEBREWS 13:8 NLT

Relationships can change. Jobs can change. You may be someone who rearranges your furniture every few months for a new look. You may change your clothes six times before deciding on an outfit. Your hair color may even change like the seasons. Change is everywhere, and although change can be good, not knowing what the future holds can be unsettling.

There is one thing, however, that is unchangeable, and that is Jesus Christ. Today, meditate on these truths about Jesus. Allow His steadfastness to give you peace in an ever-changing world:

His Word will not change (1 Peter 1:25).

His goodness will not change (Psalm 100:5).

His ways will never change (Isaiah 55:8–13).

His provision for His children will never change (Philippians 4:19).

His promises will never change (Hebrews 6:10–12).

His mercy will never change (Psalm 107:1).

His grace will never change (2 Corinthians 12:9).

His love will never change (1 Corinthians 13).

Changes will come, but Jesus will be there through each one, remaining the same always and forever.

Dear Jesus, I take comfort in knowing that You will remain the same through all the changes in my life. Amen.

Today, God Wants You to Know. . .
You Can Entrust Your Plans to Him

Commit your actions to the LORD, and your plans will succeed.
PROVERBS 16:3 NLT

At an early age, an ambitious woman planned her entire life. She determined she would earn her law degree by age twenty-five, marry by twenty-eight, become a partner in her law firm by thirty-five, and retire at fifty. She was quite disappointed when her plan failed.

Do you have any plans for your life?

The Lord desires that we have plans for our lives. He encourages us to have aspirations, goals, and hopes; however, He provides a framework for developing and implementing those plans. God wants us to develop them in cooperation with His will for us. Those plans should be in line with His plan—His overall purpose for our lives; our spiritual gifts, abilities, interests, and talents; and His perfect timing. God requires us not to hold on too tight to the plan, but rather to commit or entrust it to Him. When we surrender it to the Lord, He will secure, or "make firm," the plan. God's will cannot be thwarted; therefore, God's purpose, plan, and work will be established. There is no need to worry—just commit your plans to the Lord.

Lord, thank You that I don't need to worry about my life,
future, or plans. Help me to fully surrender to Your plan,
knowing that Your plan cannot be thwarted. Amen.

You Can Grieve with Hope

We do not want you to be uninformed about those who sleep in death,
so that you do not grieve like the rest of mankind, who have no hope.
1 THESSALONIANS 4:13 NIV

When Lazarus died and Jesus arrived at the family home, Lazarus's sister Mary ran to meet Jesus. Her grief was palpable as she fell at His feet.

"Why did you wait so long?" she sobbed. "He's gone."

Jesus knew that Mary and her brother would be reunited—very soon, in fact. However, despite this knowledge, He was visibly moved by Mary's grief. He wept. His heart ached for those He loved.

Sometimes as Christians we are given the impression that grieving or crying somehow implies that we don't trust God. That we don't believe He has everything under control. However, in 1 Thessalonians 4, when Paul teaches on the subject of death, he is clear: grieve, but not without hope. Perhaps your heart is heavy over a recent loss. Go ahead. Cry your heart out. Jesus feels your pain and your tears are precious to Him. But when you grieve, be sure to grieve with hope in the coming of our Lord.

Jesus, thank You for this beautiful picture of how very much You love us
and how You feel our pain. When I grieve, help me to do so with hope.
Amen.

Today, God Wants You to Know...
Your Conversations Impact Lives

Let no one look down on your youthfulness, but rather in speech, conduct,
love, faith and purity, show yourself an example of those who believe.
I Timothy 4:12 NASB

God hears the conversations of His children—no matter how young or old. As we spend time together and speak with one another, our Father cares about our conversations and wants them to bless and enrich the lives of those who participate.

Conversations peppered with faith and purity, as directed in 1 Timothy 4, are in stark contrast to the ungodly chatter of the world today. The world is darkened by complaints against God, cynicism, unbelief, and gossip—none of which honor God. His heart aches when we use words to tear others down rather than speak truth that encourages.

He wants us to build each other up with the words we use. True Christ-centered fellowship happens when everyone involved is encouraged and strengthened in their faith. And we must always remember that unbelievers watch and listen, always looking to find Christ in the lives of those of us who profess His name. Let's share God's faithfulness, goodness, and love, because our conversations have an impact on the lives of everyone we reach.

Jesus, please touch my lips and allow nothing dishonorable
to pass through them. Guide me and give me grace and
discernment in my conversations so that they would always
be pleasing to You and give glory to Your name. Amen.

Today, God Wants You to Know...
Your Goals Should Glorify Him

Brethren, I count not myself to have apprehended: but this one thing I do, forgetting those things which are behind, and reaching forth unto those things which are before, I press toward the mark for the prize of the high calling of God in Christ Jesus.
PHILIPPIANS 3:13–14 KJV

Many women set personal goals and priorities. Your long-term goals may include career advancement, fitness or weight loss, or some personal dream you hope to achieve. You might also have a list of short-term priorities like spending more time in God's Word, getting involved in a church ministry, or even volunteering at a local women's shelter.

New goals and priorities are always made with good intentions. At times, you may fall short of some of your goals or even neglect some of your priorities. You can, however, achieve those goals, no matter what you've done in the past. It's never too late to start over; you can accomplish anything with God's help.

As a child of God, your goals should always be those that glorify the Father. Continually strive toward the completion of your godly goals with faith and perseverance, and one day you'll reach your goals, and your eternal prize will be one of heaven's greatest rewards.

Dear God, help me to continuously aim for the dreams and goals that You've placed in my heart. Amen.

Today, God Wants You to Know...
as You Trust in Him, Your Faith Will Increase

*Now faith is confidence in what we hope
for and assurance about what we do not see.*

HEBREWS 11:1 NIV

We exercise faith in the unseen on a daily basis. When we step onto an elevator, we can't see the cables that keep us from falling. It is rare to meet the chef face-to-face when dining at a restaurant. Yet we trust the chef to prepare our food. As we shop, we use debit cards and place faith in the bank across town to back up our payments.

Christians are called to spiritual faith. God is ever-present in our lives, though we cannot see Him with our eyes. Have you found that trusting Him is easier to *talk about* than it is to *live out in daily life*?

The Lord understands the limitations of our humanity. When the disciples asked Jesus to increase their faith, His answer must have been reassuring to them: "If you have faith as small as a mustard seed, you can say to this mulberry tree, 'Be uprooted and planted in the sea,' and it will obey you" (Luke 17:6 NIV).

Surely it was not happenstance that Christ chose a seed as His example when teaching about faith. A seed has one purpose—growth. As you trust in Him and find God consistently faithful, your faith will increase.

*Father, I cannot see You with my eyes, but I know You are there.
I sense that You are at work in my life and all around me.
Increase my faith, I pray. Amen.*

Today, God Wants You to Know…

You Can Bless Him Even in the Hard Times

I bless the LORD every chance I get; my lungs expand with his praise.
PSALM 34:1 MSG

It's hard to imagine blessing God in the midst of a battle or when we're in pain. Yet He wants us to bless Him at all times: when the sink is clogged, when the bill collectors are calling, when things aren't going as planned in the workplace, when we battle discouragement or health problems. The solution to any struggle? Bless God!

There are so many ways we can bless the Lord. First, we can avoid feelings of bitterness when we're wronged. And we really bless His heart when we spend time in His Word and do what it says. When we look for the good in every person or situation, we bless God. And nature's glorious display can be a catalyst for blessing as well. A misty morning, a bird bathing, a child laughing. These are all things that evoke blessings from a thankful heart.

Make a list of all the reasons you have to bless God. Then go over that list, speaking words of thanksgiving and praise for what He's done in your life!

Lord, I have so much to be grateful for. May I never miss the little things all around me. And may I bless You—not just when things are going well but at all times! May Your praise continually be on my lips!

Today, God Wants You to Know...
He Extends Forgiveness to You

Ezra wept, prostrate in front of The Temple of God. As he
prayed and confessed, a huge number of the men, women,
and children of Israel gathered around him. All the people
were now weeping as if their hearts would break.
EZRA 10:1 MSG

Sin is not a politically correct topic these days. Yet God talks
about sin all throughout His Word. The Bible says God hates
sin and that He sent His Son to die on the cross to save us from
the results of sin—our eternal separation from God.

Sins can be "big" (murder, adultery) or "little" (gossip, envy)—
but in God's eyes, they're the same. That's why we need His sacrifice, His righteousness. Only through Jesus' death on the cross can
we be reconciled to God.

Satan loves to remind us of our sins to make us feel guilty. He
adores it when we wallow in them. But God never intended for
us to do that. Instead, God wants us to confess our sins—daily, or
hourly if need be!—receive His forgiveness, and move on to live
with renewed fervor.

What sins have separated us from God today? Let's draw near
the throne of grace so we can receive His pardon. He longs for us
to come near to Him, and He will cover us with Jesus' robe of
righteousness so that we don't have to feel guilt or shame anymore.

Lord, forgive me for the sins I've committed today. Make me ever aware
of Your grace and forgiveness so that I may share Your love with others.

People Need Him in Their Lives

*When he saw the crowds, he had compassion on them because
they were confused and helpless, like sheep without a shepherd.*
MATTHEW 9:36 NLT

Look closely at the people around you. External appearances
are deceptive. Beneath the forced smiles lie hearts that reveal
a different story. Aimless. Wandering. Lost. Many people have no
idea why they are here, what they are doing, and where they are going. Pain, fear, and anxiety are their constant companions. They are
like sheep without a shepherd.

We need the Lord's eyes to see people's hearts. Then compassion
will compel us to reach out. People need to know that they are loved
unconditionally. They need to understand that God has a purpose
for their lives. They need to realize that God can guide them along
life's journey. They need the hope of eternal life and the assurance of
a heavenly home. Putting it simply, people need the Lord.

We are all sheep in need of the Good Shepherd. Live your life
before others with authenticity and humility. Allow them to see
God's peace in times of trial, the Father's comfort in times of grief,
the Savior's hope in times of uncertainty. Be real so you can point
others to Christ. Reach out and introduce someone to the Good
Shepherd.

*Dear Lord, open my eyes to see the lost sheep around me.
May I be used to introduce them to You, the Good Shepherd. Amen.*

Today, God Wants You to Know...
He Will Grant You Wisdom

His wife's name was Abigail. And the woman
was intelligent and beautiful in appearance.
1 Samuel 25:3 nasb

Abigail is the only woman in the Bible whose brains are mentioned before her beauty. And how well she used them! She stood before a furious king and his army, calming him with just her words. She returned home at the end of the day but wisely chose just the right time to tell her quarrelsome husband the news. Her wisdom and grace made her so memorable that when her husband died, David sent for her and made her his bride.

With the stress and fast-paced lives we live today, we can easily believe that women in the Bible have little to teach us. After all, they lived thousands of years ago, without the headaches of today's world. Yet our concerns are not that different. We still worry about our families, seek to act responsibly in God's eyes, and strive to do our work with diligence.

And the wisdom to handle those concerns still comes from the same source: God. Just as He granted Abigail the wisdom to soothe a king, the Lord will grant us the wisdom and intelligence to handle whatever today's world throws at us.

All we have to do is ask.

Lord, thank You for the blessings in my life. Grant me the
wisdom and grace to deal with my family, my home, and my
work in ways that reflect my love for and faith in You. Amen.

Today, God Wants You to Know...
Strength Is Depending on Him

For thus said the Lord GOD, the Holy One of Israel, "In returning and
rest you shall be saved; in quietness and in trust shall be your strength."
ISAIAH 30:15 ESV

Assert yourself, work hard, make progress, speak up, and believe
in yourself. These are ways the world defines personal strength.
But God's Word gives a paradoxical view of strength. Rest, quietness,
and trust—these words all reflect a state of dependence.

Strength, at its core, is depending on God. Strength comes
when we acknowledge our weakness and our need for God. When
our sin overwhelms us, we repent and turn to Him for forgiveness. When we are weary of trying to earn His favor, we stop and
remember that we only have to receive His grace. In solitude, we
hear Him speak and we learn to pray. In getting to the end of our
self-reliance, we trust Him for our needs. When we are willing to
be emptied of self, then He can fill us with His life. Second Corinthians 12:9 (NKJV) says, "And He said to me, 'My grace is sufficient
for you, for My strength is made perfect in weakness.' Therefore
most gladly I will rather boast in my infirmities, that the power of
Christ may rest upon me."

What are the areas of your life in which you need to depend
more on God?

Father, remind me today that You are not asking me to be strong,
but to depend on You. In my weakness, You will be strong.
Help me to return, rest, listen, and trust.

Today, God Wants You to Know...

No One's Love for You Can Compare to His

For we do not have a high priest who is unable to empathize with our weaknesses, but we have one who has been tempted in every way, just as we are—yet he did not sin. Let us then approach God's throne of grace with confidence, so that we may receive mercy and find grace to help us in our time of need.

HEBREWS 4:15–16 NIV

There is no one like a sister. Whether or not you have a female sibling, you have undoubtedly discovered a sister along life's journey. A sister is someone who "gets you." When you succeed, she cheers; when you fail, she is there to help pick up the pieces. When you are in need, you don't have to beg her for help. She feels your hurt and wants to help you in any way that she can. Sometimes a sister understands you even better than a parent because she is closer to your age and has walked through some of the same things you are experiencing.

Even a sister's love cannot compare to Christ's love. However you're struggling, help is available through Jesus. Our Savior walked on this earth for thirty-three years. He was fully God *and* fully man. He got dirt under His fingernails. He felt hunger. He knew weakness. He was tempted. He felt tired. He "gets it."

Go boldly before the throne of grace as a daughter of God. Pray in Jesus' name for an outpouring of His grace and mercy in your life.

Father, I ask You boldly in the name of Christ to help me. Amen.

Today, God Wants You to Know...
He Is the Conductor of
the Symphony of Your Life

By day the LORD *directs his love, at night his song
is with me—a prayer to the God of my life.*
PSALM 42:8 NIV

Have you ever thought of your life as being like a symphony?
There are some high highs and some low lows. There are
crescendo moments, when everything seems to fall into place, and
there are some pianissimo moments, when things draw to a quiet
stillness. And in the midst of it all, there is the Conductor, standing
with baton in hand, directing. He calls the shots. He tells the musi-
cians when to play furiously and when to slow to a halt.

God is the director of your life. During the daytime—when
most of the major decisions of life are made—He's there, leading
you, guiding you. And at night, when His direction might not be so
clear, His song plays over you.

Today, begin to see your life as a symphony with many move-
ments. Allow the Lord—your Conductor—to lead you through
the highs and lows, the crescendo moments and the pianissimo
ones. Then when night shadows fall, listen closely for the song He's
playing over you.

*Oh Father! I can almost hear the music now. Thank You for
the reminder that my life is a symphony and You are the Conductor.
I don't want to carry the baton, Lord. Remove it from my hands.
Direct me in the daytime and sing Your song over me at night.*

Today, God Wants You to Know...
in an Ever-Changing World,
He Remains the Same

Jesus Christ is the same yesterday and today and forever.
Hebrews 13:8 NIV

The world and our lives are constantly changing. Some of this is due to outside circumstances—war, inflation, job loss, death. And some is self-imposed. We change our careers for something more challenging. As our clothes wear out, we buy new ones. When we gain weight, we take an exercise class to lose a few pounds.

No matter what changes are happening in our lives, we can rest assured that Jesus Christ remains the same—yesterday, today, and forever. Minute by minute, we can look to Him for guidance, reassurance, and peace of mind. We can rest in the fact that Jesus, our Rock, is always there, waiting to strengthen us and give us the relief we crave.

No matter how bleak the world looks, no matter what crisis we are going through, we do not have to worry, for although heaven and earth may pass away, God's words—the anchor of our spirit, the bread of our lives, that which gives us peace beyond understanding—will remain forever.

Ah, Lord, what a relief to know that in this ever-changing world, You remain the same. You are always there, waiting for me to come to You, loving me and sheltering me. Thank You for being my Rock, my Refuge, and my Rest. Amen.

He Can Help Curb Your Unhealthy Cravings

> *I decide to do good, but I don't really do it; I decide not to
> do bad, but then I do it anyway. My decisions, such as they are,
> don't result in actions. Something has gone wrong deep
> within me and gets the better of me every time.*
> ROMANS 7:18–20 MSG

We women love our chocolate. Maybe if we consumed it only in pure cocoa form it would be good for us, but most of us love it with sugar and fat added and could eat it every day. Of course, our taste buds also may like broccoli, but unlike chocolate, we prefer it in small doses.

You might find yourself feasting daily on fears, worries, jealousies, and stress—the fat-laden chocolate of life. And just as we know we should eat good foods like broccoli, we know love, forgiveness, patience, and self-control are good for us, but most of us struggle to consume enough of them to keep our spiritual life healthy.

What we need is discipline in our spiritual (and physical) diet, but we can't do it on our own. We need God's power to help us crave those things that are the healthiest. Through prayer and biblical guidance, it is possible to change our taste buds to want the things that are the best for our bodies and souls.

> *Lord, help me to feed my body and soul the things
> that will keep me healthiest and most useful to You.
> Help me to crave the things that are best for me.*

Today, God Wants You to Know. . .
When You're in over Your Head, He'll Be There

God, God, save me! I'm in over my head.
PSALM 69:1 MSG

The bills have piled up almost as high as the laundry. You got a traffic ticket. You lost your keys or dropped your cell phone in the bathtub. People in your life are too busy to listen, and you are too busy to listen to them. It's raining. It's pouring. You stand drenched to the bone and begin to shiver in the cold. Tears start to flow down your cheeks, but no one notices. The tears just mingle with the rain, and maybe everyone else is crying also. We are all too busy, too stressed, too frazzled.

"God, God, save me! I'm in over my head," the psalmist wrote. And in the twenty-first century, we can relate to his plea!

Come, Father, and lift from me these burdens I've created for myself. Help me to shed some extra burdens in order that I might focus again on what's important, which is You, my God. Help me to rest in Your goodness and Your deep love for me.

I am in over my head! I cry out to You. I need You this day, this hour, this moment. I need the One who made me and knit me together in my mother's womb to find me here. I need You to save me—if even from myself.

Father, there are times I cannot do one more thing.
I realize I have lost You in the shuffle. Find me, I pray. Amen.

You Can Go to Him with Childlike Faith

Jesus called the children to him and said, "Let the
little children come to me, and do not hinder them,
for the kingdom of God belongs to such as these."
LUKE 18:16 NIV

Jesus loved children. He even taught His disciples a lesson using them as an illustration: in order to enter the kingdom of God, one must receive Him like a little child.

What is childlike faith? It's an innocent, fearless faith a child places in his mom and dad. It's a kind of pure, unsoiled trust that leaves no room for distrust or sarcasm. Childlike faith doesn't have to be accompanied by a ton of Bible knowledge. A simple "I believe Jesus is the Christ, the Son of God" is all it requires.

This is the kind of faith Christ desires in those seeking Him. Once you become a follower of Christ, you will begin to grow in faith and learn to put your complete trust in God and His Word.

Jesus loves all His children. You can always depend on Him. His arms will always be there to hold you and to keep you safe. Go to Him with childlike faith, with no fear or doubts.

Dear Jesus, I'm so glad that I'm Your child. Help me to
always have that childlike faith that is pleasing to You. Amen.

Today, God Wants You to Know...

Your Mission in Life Is to Make a Difference for Him

The life of mortals is like grass, they flourish like
a flower of the field; the wind blows over it and
it is gone, and its place remembers it no more.
PSALM 103:15–16 NIV

Here lies Jane Doe.

She kept an insanely full schedule.

If we're really honest with ourselves, we would admit that we'd all like to contribute something lasting to this world. But what kind of impact are we making and what kind of legacy are we leaving? Apart from God, no one and nothing else will matter.

Think about past rulers, dictators, and presidents. At one point in time, they were some of the most powerful people in the world. Today we can't name even half of them, let alone remember what they did or didn't do. What they gave their lives for may not have any meaning now.

Our lives begin and end in the blink of an eye. The things that we think are so important may one day be merely trivial. All that will matter is that we told others about Christ. Our mission is to do the will of God, to go where God is working, and to make a difference for Him.

Lord, I am willing to make an eternal difference for You. Amen.

He Places Opportunities in Your Life

"Who knows? Maybe you were made queen for just such a time as this."
ESTHER 4:14 MSG

To live in the center of God's will—to walk, step-by-step, the path He's prepared before us—is no easy task. At some point in our lives, we each wonder, *Why am I here? What did God make me to do?*

Too often we look for the big Hollywood blockbuster answer: *I will find a cure for cancer. I will solve world hunger. I will save thirty-eight children from a burning school bus.* While these things are possible, they're unlikely to happen to most of us.

Instead, God wants us to be sensitive to the opportunities He places in our lives—sometimes on a daily basis—to make a difference for His kingdom. Do you see someone who needs a good meal or just someone to talk to? Could you help out a coworker who is burdened with a heavy workload? Big or small, the choices we make to help others are just one part of the puzzle that is the meaning of life.

Like Queen Esther in the Old Testament, we need to examine our daily lives and consider. . .maybe God brought us to this very place for such a time as this.

Father, please show me the purpose for my day today.
Open my eyes to the opportunities that You put before
me to make a difference in other people's lives.

Today, God Wants You to Know...
No One Is Unlovable

"Love one another,
even as I have loved you."
JOHN 13:34 NASB

In a society that has distorted the concept of love, it's reassuring to know that God loves us with a deep, limitless love. He is, in fact, love itself. He gave His Son to die for people who didn't love Him in return. God the Father even had to turn His face from His Son when He died, as He took the sin of humankind upon Himself. What incredible love that is!

We Christians tell Jesus we love Him, and His response is, "I love you more." We cannot comprehend that kind of love, yet we are the recipients of it. And He loves us not because of anything we've done, but because of His goodness. First John 4:19 (KJV) says, "We love him, because he first loved us."

Jesus also commands us to love others in the same way that He loves us. We all have unlovable people in our lives. But Jesus doesn't see anyone as unlovable. Look at that difficult-to-love person through new eyes today and love her as God has loved you.

Heavenly Father, thank You for Your love for me.
Forgive me for not loving others in that same way.
Give me the ability to love others as You have instructed. Amen.

Today, God Wants You to Know...
He Turns Impossibilities into Possibilities

*Jesus replied, "What is impossible
with man is possible with God."*
LUKE 18:27 NIV

Have you ever lived through what appeared to be an impossible circumstance? Maybe it was starting over after a divorce or living through the loss of a loved one or surviving a devastating disease or facing a mortgage payment when you knew the money just wasn't there.

Webster defines the word *impossible* as "not capable of being, being done, or happening." As a Christian, you should know how Jesus defines the word. According to Luke 18:27, there are things that are impossible with people. But with God on your side, there is absolutely nothing that is impossible. No matter how difficult your problem may look, always remember that God can turn impossibilities into possibilities.

Are you facing a situation that seems totally impossible? Friend, don't dwell on your problem or circumstance. Instead, look only to God, who makes all things possible. Put your complete trust in Him and His Word, and remove the word *impossible* from your vocabulary.

*Dear God, I know nothing is impossible with You. I choose
to put my complete trust in You and Your Word. Amen.*

Today, God Wants You to Know...
He Will Help You Achieve Your Dreams

"What no eye has seen, what no ear has heard,
and what no human mind has conceived"—
the things God has prepared for those who love him.
1 CORINTHIANS 2:9 NIV

Dreams, goals, and expectations are part of our daily lives. We have an idea of what we want and how we're going to achieve it. Disappointment can raise its ugly head when what we wanted—what we expected—doesn't happen like we thought it should or doesn't happen as fast as we planned.

Disappointment can lead to doubt. Perhaps questions tempt you to doubt the direction you felt God urging you to pursue. Don't quit! Don't give up! Press on with your dream. Failure isn't failure until you quit. When it looks like it's over, stand strong. With God's assistance, there is another way, a higher plan, or a better time to achieve your dream.

God knows the dreams He has placed inside of you. He created you and knows what you can do—even better than you know yourself. Maintain your focus—not on the dream but on the Dream Maker—and together you will achieve your dream.

God, thank You for putting dreams in my heart. I refuse to quit.
I'm looking to You to show me how to reach my dreams. Amen.

You Are Created in His Image

When you tell God you'll do something, do it—now.
God takes no pleasure in foolish gabble. Vow it, then do it.
Far better not to vow in the first place than to vow and not pay up.
ECCLESIASTES 5:4–5 MSG

Have you ever known people who made promises they didn't keep? Maybe they said they would call, but didn't. Perhaps they promised a lunch together or a movie, then simply got busy and forgot. It's frustrating, isn't it? A person like that is hard to trust. And when you have to work with someone who doesn't follow through, it can be even more frustrating.

How wonderful that God never forgets His promises. If He says it, He means it. And if He means it, He does it. Talk about keeping your word! God is the very epitome of trustworthiness.

Remember that you are created in God's image, and He's all about honesty. So pray before making commitments; then do what you've said you would do. And when the Lord speaks into your life, giving you instruction—like ministering to someone in need or spending more time in the Word—get to it! Be a woman of your word—both to people and to the Lord.

Lord, I want to be known as a woman of my word. I want to
be trustworthy. Today, remind me of the commitments I've made;
then set me back on the right track to get those things done.

Today, God Wants You to Know...
He Has the Power to Help You Press On

Create in me a pure heart, O God, and renew a steadfast
spirit within me. Do not cast me from your presence or take
your Holy Spirit from me. Restore to me the joy of your
salvation and grant me a willing spirit, to sustain me.
PSALM 51:10–12 NIV

Perseverance. Some days that word sounds so difficult. Maybe you dread Mondays, knowing that a full week of work and errands and demands awaits you. Maybe mornings in general are tough, each day holding burdens of its own.

Do not grow weary. Strive each day to keep a pure heart. Don't complain or dwell on small annoyances. Recognize your own worth in God's eyes, and recognize the worth of others as well. Be joyful, even when you are not particularly happy.

This world will do all it can to pull you down, to tell you to give up. When you're tempted to grow discouraged, remember that you stand in the presence of God and that He has given you the gift of His Spirit for times such as these.

Ask God for the power to press forward when your own spirit grows tired. Turn to other Christian believers for encouragement. Know that you are not alone—that you will never be alone. God craves your devotion. Turn to Him, and persevere.

Lord, forgive me for being shortsighted and feeling overwhelmed
by the worries of this world. Remind me of Your grace and salvation.
Remind me of Your love for me so that I might better love others.

Today, God Wants You to Know…

You Can Be a Blessing to Those Around You

As a father has compassion on his children,
so the LORD has compassion on those who fear him.
PSALM 103:13 NIV

What does it mean that God has compassion on us? For some women, it means that God gives strength as they battle a chronic illness. For others, it means that He has forgotten their sins, because they came to Christ from a life of deep regrets.

How do you need God to show you His compassion today? Do you need guidance for a decision? Ask Him, and He will show you what to do. Perhaps you long for a companion to talk to. He is always available. Maybe you believe that God couldn't love you because you've strayed from Him. Remember that He is the image of the loving father who ran to his prodigal son when he returned.

Another wonderful aspect of God's compassion is that once we've experienced it, we long to share it with others. So when you feel that God has met your needs, ask Him how you can be a blessing to the people around you. Does a coworker need some encouragement? Or maybe your best friend could use some girl time. If you ask Him, God will give you fresh ideas for ministering compassion to those in your circle of influence.

Lord, I am so thankful for—and in awe of—Your compassion.
Help me spread it to everyone I know.

Today, God Wants You to Know...
He Is Just a Prayer Away

Cast your burden upon the LORD and He will sustain you;
He will never allow the righteous to be shaken.
PSALM 55:22 NASB

When we have a problem, our first thought is to contact a friend. In our world today, with so many technological advances, it is easy to communicate even with people who are far away. Just a hundred years ago, people waited days to receive a message from another town!

Certainly God desires that we help to bear one another's burdens and that we seek wise counsel. The trouble is that in doing so, often we fail to take our burdens to the One who can do something about them. We are called to release our cares to our heavenly Father. A cause with an effect is implied in Psalm 55:22—*If* you cast your burden on Him, *then* He will sustain you.

Sustain is defined by Webster as a verb meaning "to strengthen or support physically or mentally" or "to bear the weight of an object." Does it sound inviting to have the sovereign God of the universe strengthen and support you? Would it help if He bore the weight of your current trial? Our sovereign God is there when heartaches are taking their toll. He doesn't have a cell phone or an e-mail address, but He is always just a prayer away.

Lift the worries that weigh on my mind and heart today, Father.
I can't bear them alone any longer. In my weakness, You are strong.
Thank You for Your promise to sustain me. Amen.

Sometimes It's Okay—and Necessary—to Say No

> *Keep a close watch on how you live and on your teaching.*
> *Stay true to what is right for the sake of your own*
> *salvation and the salvation of those who hear you.*
> 1 TIMOTHY 4:16 NLT

Every woman needs to guard her time wisely—whether single or married. We are all in danger of getting exhausted running here and there to do all the things that are seemingly good and intended to bring glory to God.

So before agreeing to take on a volunteer position, recall how flight attendants remind airline passengers in the event of an emergency to secure their own oxygen masks before helping others around them. In many ways God tries to tell us this also as He reminds us not to neglect our time in prayer, study, and fellowship with Him. If our spiritual oxygen isn't flowing from a full tank, our ability to assist others will run out and we'll become useless.

Securing our own mask first sometimes means saying "no" to groups that see us as "singularly" available and "yes" to God, who truly requires our time. Only then will we be alert and equipped to serve others in His strength.

> *Dear Lord, help me to prioritize my schedule so I can*
> *be refreshed and energized by time with You and in*
> *turn be inspired to do the tasks You place before me.*

Today, God Wants You to Know...
He Will Be a Source of Peace and Harmony in Your Home

My people will live in a peaceful habitation,
and in secure dwellings and in undisturbed resting places.
ISAIAH 32:18 NASB

Home is where you should feel safe and most free to be yourself—a place of refuge from the outside world. Your home should reflect a strength and quiet confidence welcoming to your family, friends, and God.

The atmosphere of your home starts with you. It takes a conscious effort and true discipline to leave the world's cares at the threshold of the front door and stay committed to the pursuit of a peaceful home.

Perhaps you've been running all day and you need to slow down. Take a few minutes before you enter your home and find your focus. Let go of the day: Shake off the frustration of work, school, relational, and financial concerns. Make a decision to be proactive and peaceful instead of reactive and defensive.

Then step across the threshold into a place of peace. Put a smile on your face and make a deliberate effort to relax. Speak to your family in a soft, positive, encouraging voice. You set the tone of your home, and you control the pace within it. Make it a place of peace today.

Lord, thank You for reminding me to cast off the cares of the day.
Help me to bring peace, harmony, and unity into my home. Amen.

Today, God Wants You to Know...
He Intended for You to Experience Joy

"The joy of the LORD is your strength."
NEHEMIAH 8:10 NIV

In our success-driven world, fun is an often-overlooked commodity. There's a corporate ladder to climb, a glass ceiling to break through, another committee meeting to attend. Serious, staid, and structured, our lives lack joy. We race a clock with a sweeping second hand.

Paul exhorted the Christian community to be full of joy *now*. The Psalms encourage us to sing and dance and praise His name. How is that possible with a solemn face? A little lighthearted fun releases pent-up tension and balances life's scales. Laughter will lower our blood pressure. That cheerful heart is good medicine.

Surely it's time for a bit of spontaneity. First Thessalonians 5:16 (NIV) says to "be joyful always." In our cyberspace world, we can share jokes and hilarious videos. Pull one up on the screen, throw back your head, and laugh. Realize God intended for us to have joy in our lives. Say, "Yes, Lord," and chuckle.

Father, I live in a world loaded with danger, serious issues, and worry.
Help me to find joy in my life this day. Amen.

You Can Talk to Him on Behalf of Others

*"I looked for someone among them who would build up
the wall and stand before me in the gap on behalf of the
land so I would not have to destroy it, but I found no one."*

 EZEKIEL 22:30 NIV

Each prayer request you offer up to God is important to you,
and when you ask others to pray, you're counting on them to
help carry you through the tough times.

Do you give the same consideration to those who ask you for
prayer? It's easy in the busyness of life to overlook a request someone else has made. Maybe you don't know the person very well or
you don't really have an understanding of the situation. Perhaps
the request came in an e-mail that you quickly glanced at and then
deleted. Yet even with e-mailed prayer requests, others trust you to
stand in the gap for them during difficult times in their lives.

Don't delay. Take time right when you receive a request to talk
to the Lord on the requester's behalf. Be the bridge that carries that
person through the valley of darkness back to the mountaintop of joy.

*Heavenly Father, help me to have a heart of compassion for those
I know and even for those I don't know who need Your comfort
and love. Help me never to be too busy to pray for them. Amen.*

Today, God Wants You to Know...
Godly Characteristics Will Make You Shine!

Therefore, as God's chosen people, holy and dearly loved, clothe yourselves
with compassion, kindness, humility, gentleness and patience.
COLOSSIANS 3:12 NIV

We all spend time selecting what to wear each day. Sometimes it is simply a matter of what is clean (or can at least be resurrected from the dirty clothes hamper!).

Some women are trendy, which requires them to keep up with the latest fashions. Others are more practical as they piece together a week's worth of outfits with just a couple of pairs of neutral-colored pants and some solid-colored tops.

Clothing is important. It says something about a person. Think about a black-tie affair, an interview, a tennis match, or a day on the beach. Each calls for a different type of attire. To show up on the beach in a tuxedo or at the tennis match in a business suit would be ridiculous!

As believers, God tells us to clothe ourselves with compassion, kindness, humility, gentleness, and patience. These traits cannot be found in a department store or in the latest fashion magazine. They come only from the Holy Spirit living in and through us.

Today as you choose the clothing you will wear, choose also to clothe yourself with godly characteristics that will cause you to shine as a daughter of the Lord.

God, it is not always easy to be kind or compassionate.
Sometimes humility, gentleness, and especially patience are also
difficult. Help me to be certain I am fully clothed with these
attitudes before I leave home each morning. Amen.

There Is Power in a Simple Touch

She thought, "If I just touch his clothes, I will be healed."
MARK 5:28 NIV

We should never underestimate the power of touch. In our busy lives, as we rush from one appointment to another, skimping on affection with our families and loved ones can become routine. We wave good-bye to our children without stopping for a hug. Husbands head off to work with the barest brush of a kiss.

We do our loved ones a disservice, however, when we skip touching them. Touching communicates our affection but also our affirmation and sympathy. You can encourage people—or comfort them—with a simple touch. The Bible records Jesus touching many people, comforting and healing them. He also let people touch Him, such as the sinful woman who touched and kissed His feet (Luke 7:38).

In Mark 5, however, the true power of a simple touch is beautifully portrayed. This woman who had suffered for so long believed so strongly in Jesus that she knew the quickest touch of His hem would heal her. She reached out, and her faith made her well.

So hold those you love close. Hug them, and let them see a bit of Jesus' love in you every day.

Lord, I turn to You when I need comfort. Let me also offer those around me the comfort of a loving touch. Amen.

Today, God Wants You to Know...
Your Spirit Can Draw Others to Him

Everywhere we go, people breathe in the exquisite fragrance. Because of Christ, we give off a sweet scent rising to God, which is recognized by those on the way of salvation—an aroma redolent with life.

2 CORINTHIANS 2:15–16 MSG

Smells are all around us. The aroma of lavender relaxes us, the scent of coffee jump-starts us, and the odor of a skunk offends us.

Have you ever considered how a person's spirit has an aroma? When you meet someone who is godly, gentle, and sincerely kind, that person's spirit seems to exude an inviting aroma like home-baked cookies or mulled apple cider that draws others in. But there are also people you meet who almost immediately seem to give off a sharp odor like vinegar or ammonia. They have an unsettled spirit in which bitterness and discontent are cultivated.

What kind of scent do you want your spirit to emanate? Remember that it has the power to change a room and even a whole community.

So as you perform your daily hygiene, putting perfume on your skin, consider also your spiritual perfume. Keep the scent fresh, not overpowering, and welcoming by keeping your spirit in line with the Spirit of God through prayer, Bible study, and praise.

Holy Spirit, I welcome You into my life. Be a perfume that proves to others that You are sovereign in my life and that draws them to Jesus Christ.

Today, God Wants You to Know...
He Is the Way, the Truth, and the Life

In him was life, and that life was the light of all mankind.
JOHN 1:4 NIV

Do you have a life?

You've probably been asked that more than once. Having a life usually means you have a busy social calendar, lots of places to go, things to do, and friends to hang out with. The world tells us that those are the things that bring happiness and fulfillment. The Bible defines having a life a bit differently.

In John 14:6 Jesus tells us that He is the way, the truth, and the life. He is our only way to our Father in heaven. Jesus is the light of the world and the only One who can fill us with life. Real life. Deep fulfillment. A life that makes a difference and lasts for eternity.

So do you have the light of Christ living inside you, or do you need to get a life? A place to go, things to do, and people to see don't mean a whole lot at the end of your life here on earth. You will never look back and wish you could have attended one more social event.

Jesus is the only way to eternal life. Make sure you've got a life before you leave!

Dear Jesus, I want You to light up my soul and give me eternal life.
Help me to live my life for You. Amen.

Today, God Wants You to Know...

Your Job Is to Love Him, Love Others—
Enough Said!

*Jesus replied: " 'Love the Lord your God with all your heart and
with all your soul and with all your mind.' This is the first and greatest
commandment. And the second is like it: 'Love your neighbor as yourself.'
All the Law and the Prophets hang on these two commandments."*

MATTHEW 22:37–40 NIV

Love God and love people. The whole of the Gospel can be
summed up in these two statements. Jesus taught us how to
love. He demonstrated it by giving all of Himself for others. And
His love for the Father was evident in everything He did.

When we love God with our whole heart, it just comes
naturally to love people. And we're told to love them as we love
ourselves. Think about that for a moment. How much do you love
yourself? Enough to make sure all of your needs are met, right?
Imagine that kind of love expressed to a friend. It's a pouring-
yourself-out kind of love.

It's interesting to note that Jesus says, "All the Law and the
Prophets hang on these two commandments." He's really saying,
"What's the point of all of the other stuff if you don't have love?" That's
a question we need to consider today. What's the point of going to
church, giving financially, teaching Bible studies, or directing the
children's ministry if you don't truly love those you come in contact
with on a daily basis? So go forth and love!

*Father, I want to acknowledge how much I love You with all my heart,
soul, mind, and strength. Help me to love others as I love myself.*

Today, God Wants You to Know...
You Are the Apple of His Eye

For thus says the LORD of hosts: "He...
who touches you touches the apple of His eye."
ZECHARIAH 2:8 NKJV

The apple of the eye refers to the pupil—the very center, or heart, of the eye. Consider the lengths we go to in order to protect our eyes. We wear protective glasses in some workplaces. We close our eyes or squint in windstorms or bright light. When dust blows, we turn our heads or put up our hands to keep the dirt from ending up in our eyes.

When we do get something in an eye, the ache and discomfort are instant. Tears form, and we seek to get the particle out as quickly as possible to stop the pain. If we are unable to remove the offending bit, we often become unable to do anything but focus on the discomfort.

To think that we are the apple of God's eye is incredible. Consider the care He must take for us. He will go to great lengths to protect us from harm. When something or someone does attack us, God feels our pain. He is instantly aware of our discomfort, for it is His own. When the storms of life come, we must remember how God feels each twinge of suffering. Despite the adversity, we can praise God, for He is sheltering us.

Thank You, God, that You are so aware of what is happening to me.
Thank You for Your protection. Amen.

Today, God Wants You to Know...
He Is Bigger Than Any Storm You Face

*The eternal God is your refuge,
and underneath are the everlasting arms.*
DEUTERONOMY 33:27 NIV

Stressful issues face us each day. Whether it's work, school, or the neighbors next door, there's always some problem to deal with. And when these bumps in the road arise, our natural tendency is to worry, fret, and be anxious. Not only is that attitude counterproductive, but God's Word says it's disobedient. Scripture directs us to turn our worries over to our heavenly Father and rest in Him. To fret is wrong.

Hannah Whitall Smith said, "There are two things which are more utterly incompatible even than oil and water, and these two are trust and worry." We must trust in a God who is able to do all things. We must trust in a God who cares. We must trust in a God with whom we may have a personal relationship. The Bible says so.

When life's storms are overwhelming, we should take our troubles to Him and seek protection from the One who cannot be moved. Climb into the Father's lap and feel His embrace. He is still in heaven and cares about His beloved children. He is our refuge. He's bigger than any storm we might face.

*Dear Lord, I admit worry turns my attention from You.
Help me realize You are ever present and will care for me. Amen.*

Today, God Wants You to Know...
He Will Bring You Healing

Behold, I will bring it health and healing; I will heal them
and reveal to them the abundance of peace and truth.
JEREMIAH 33:6 NKJV

Our health—physical, mental, emotional, and spiritual—is important to God. He longs to see us whole in every area of our lives. As believers in His grace and goodness, we ought to be diligent about seeking health so that we can be good stewards of His gifts.

If we confess our sins to God, He will bring relief to our souls. When we're distressed, we have Jesus, the Prince of Peace, to give us peace. When our emotions threaten to overwhelm us, we can implore Jehovah Rapha—the God Who Heals—to calm our anxious hearts. When we're physically sick, we can cry out to Jesus, our Great Physician. While He may not always heal us in the ways we might like, He will always give us strength, courage, and peace.

So whether our problems affect us physically, spiritually, mentally, or emotionally, we can trust that God will come to us and bring us healing. And beyond our temporal lives, we can look forward with hope to our heavenly lives. There we will be healthy, whole, and alive—forever.

Jehovah Rapha, thank You for healing me. Help me do my part
to seek health and the abundance of peace and truth You provide.

Today, God Wants You to Know...

He Is the Living Water and the Bread of Life

*Just as the living Father sent me and I live because of the Father,
so the one who feeds on me will live because of me.*
JOHN 6:57 NIV

Have you ever stood in front of the refrigerator eating something that doesn't even taste that good? Have you found yourself staring at a closet full of clothes you hardly ever wear? You make resolutions and muster up willpower, but time and again you eat too much or buy too many things you don't need and that don't satisfy your desire. Perhaps you are trying to satisfy soul hunger with physical things.

What are you really hungry for? What are you seeking through the things you overindulge in? Jesus said He is the living water and the bread of life. Water and food satisfy basic appetites. Jesus alone satisfies our deepest desires and needs.

Seek Him. Ask Him to satisfy your heart. Ask Him for a desire to know Him, and receive His love for you. He will give you a hunger and thirst for His presence in your life. That is His will for you, and you can be sure He will answer that prayer.

*Christ Jesus, give me a desire for You. Help me
examine my soul hunger and turn to You to fill it.*

Today, God Wants You to Know...

He Is Waiting—and Wanting— to Do Everyday Life with You

"And the one who sent me is with me—he has not deserted me.
For I always do what pleases him."

JOHN 8:29 NLT

We lose things on a daily basis. Each year we probably spend hours looking for things—keys, sunglasses, lipstick, or even the saltshaker that normally rests next to the stove. We know these items don't sprout wings and walk off but have been set somewhere and forgotten by you or someone you know.

You are God's most prized possession, and while He'll never forget where you are, sometimes we walk off from Him. We lose ourselves in the things we need to do, the places we need to go, and the people we need to see. Our calendars fill up with commitments we're obligated to keep. We often commit to too many things and exhaust ourselves trying to stay ahead of our schedules.

The further we displace ourselves from God—not necessarily on purpose—the more we become lost in our own space. While we're doing life on our own, we can forget that He is standing there waiting to do life every day with us. If you feel distant from Him today, look up. He's waiting for you to find your rightful place with Him.

God, I never want to become so busy that I lose sight of You.
Show me what things I should commit to and what things
are for someone else to do, so that I am available to You and
ready to serve in the capacity You've prepared me for. Amen.

Everyone in the Body of Christ Has a Place and a Purpose

He makes the whole body fit together perfectly. As each part does its own special work, it helps the other parts grow, so that the whole body is healthy and growing and full of love.
EPHESIANS 4:16 NLT

Have you ever put together a really large jigsaw puzzle? Maybe you struggled to get all the pieces to fit in place. Some were obvious and others were a challenge.

The body of Christ is a lot like a giant puzzle. It's filled with many, many pieces, and they all fit together seamlessly to form the most beautiful picture on earth—more beautiful than any seascape or mountain peak.

Each piece in a puzzle is critical to the whole. Sure, when you look at them individually, you might wonder, "How in the world can this piece fit? It doesn't look like any of the others. It's not shaped like any of the others." Still, it fits! And when you see it in its proper place, it makes perfect sense.

This is a great day to praise the Lord for the many puzzle pieces—Christian brothers and sisters—you've been given. Think about the ones in the farthest reaches of the earth. They're all a part of this glorious picture that makes up the church.

Oh Lord, I'm so grateful that everyone in the body of Christ has a place. Thank You for fitting us together so beautifully. And thank You that we've each been given our own job to do. May I learn to do mine well so that others might grow in You.

Today, God Wants You to Know...

When You Forgive, You Will Be Forgiven

"If you hold anything against anyone, forgive [her],
so that your Father in heaven may forgive you your sins."
MARK 11:25 NIV

Good friendships—those few girls you chat with on the phone, go with to the mall, or have a cup of coffee with—are wonderful. At some point, though, one of these close friends may hurt you with her words or actions.

You may have a friend who wounded you deeply. Have you forgiven her? *But she never asked for forgiveness!* you may be thinking. Even so, Jesus tells us to forgive. It may seem impossible to obey His command, but He can help you.

God sent His only Son to die for our sins. If anyone can identify with the pain of being offended, it's Him! But He willingly forgave, and we are to follow His example. God tells us in His Word that He will remember our sins "no more" (Hebrews 10:17 NIV) when we ask His forgiveness. We may always remember being offended by a friend, but He promises that He will put our offenses out of His mind and never bring them up again. How wonderful to be forgiven—and to forgive!

Lord Jesus, thank You for forgiving me. Please help me to
extend that forgiveness to others, even if they don't ask.
And help me to do my best to forget the offense. Amen.

His Word Is Comfort Food for Your Soul

*For whatever things were written before were
written for our learning, that we through the patience
and comfort of the Scriptures might have hope.*
ROMANS 15:4 NKJV

A big mound of ice cream topped with hot fudge; a full bowl
of salty, buttery popcorn; grilled cheese sandwiches and
warm chicken noodle soup fixed by Mom—comfort food. There is
nothing like a generous helping of things that bring the sensation
of comfort to a worn body at the end of a long day or to a bruised
mind after a disappointment. Those comfort foods soothe the body
and mind because, through the senses, they remind us of happier
and more secure times.

Romans 15:4 tells us that the scriptures are comfort food for the
soul. They were written and given so that, through our learning, we
would be comforted with the truths of God. Worldly pleasures bring
a temporary comfort, but the problem still remains when the pleasure or comfort fades. However, the words of God are soothing and
provide permanent hope and peace. Through God's Word, you will
be changed, and your troubles will dim in the bright light of Christ.
So the next time you are sad, lonely, or disappointed, before you turn
to pizza, turn to the Word of God as your source of comfort.

*Thank You, Father, for the rich comfort Your Word provides.
Help me to remember to find my comfort in scripture rather than
through earthly things that will ultimately fail me. Amen.*

Today, God Wants You to Know...
He Wants to Be a Part of Your Life

What is man that You are mindful of him,
and the son of man that You visit him?
PSALM 8:4 NKJV

What are you thinking about today? Do you have a list of things you want to get done, people you need to call, or maybe a vacation you want to plan? Your thoughts fill up your days and keep you busy going and doing life.

Have you ever wondered what God thinks about? He thinks about you! You are always on His mind. In all you think and do, He considers you and makes intercession for you. He knows the thoughts and intents of your heart. He understands you like no other person can. He knows your strengths and weaknesses, your darkest fears and highest hopes. He's constantly aware of your feelings and how you interact with or without Him each day.

God is always with you, waiting for you to remember Him—to call on Him for help, for friendship, for anything you need. He wants to be a big part of your life. And if you include Him, He will open the doors to as much goodness, mercy, and love as you'll allow Him to bless you with.

Lord, help me to remember You as I go throughout my day. I want to include You in my life and always be thinking of You, too. Amen.

He Will Fill Your Cup to Overflowing

O God, thou art my God; early will I seek thee.
PSALM 63:1 KJV

It is early morning and we stumble from our beds to take a shower, apply makeup, and blow-dry our hair. Meanwhile, coffee brews in the kitchen, and with a yawn we fill our cups. Busy women have limited time to relax, reflect, and pray. Yet a different and more significant type of cup longs to be filled—our spirit.

King David reigned over the nation of Israel and was responsible for all that that entailed. Yet he found time to seek the counsel, mercy, and direction of God daily. The more responsibilities he assumed, the more he prayed and meditated on God's precepts. Well before David was inundated with worldly concerns, nagging obligations, and his administrative duties, the Bible suggests that he sought the Lord in the early morning hours.

If the king of Israel recognized his need to spend time with God, how much more should we? When we seek our heavenly Father before daily activities demand our attention, the Holy Spirit regenerates our spirits, and our cups overflow.

Dear Lord, I take this time to pray and spend time with You before I attend to daily responsibilities. Fill my cup with the presence and power of Your Spirit. Give me the wisdom and direction I need today. Amen.

Today, God Wants You to Know...
You Can Give All Your Baggage to Him

Give all your worries and cares to God, for he cares about you.
1 PETER 5:7 NLT

Imagine that your best friend has announced she's treating you to an all-expenses-paid cruise. All of your meals are included, and she's even throwing in a brand-new wardrobe.

"Leave your bags behind," she tells you. "All you have to do is show up."

Can you imagine arriving at the cruise ship with suitcases full of clothes, shoes, and food? "Why are you carrying all this junk?" your friend would say. "I told you I had it covered—don't you trust me?"

All too often, this is how we approach God. He invites us to give Him our burdens, but we show up, time and time again, weighed down with bags so full we can't even carry them. So we drag them behind us wherever we go. They slow us down so that we're not productive, just burdened. Worry, anger, resentment, anxious thoughts. . . Sometimes the list is long.

God has told us to give all of our cares to Him. He promises that He has them covered, and yet we still hang on. What baggage are you carrying today that you can give to the Lord?

Father, thank You for the invitation to cast all my cares upon You. Help me to let go of the things that are weighing me down and to trust You to take them for me.

Today, God Wants You to Know...
You Are Safe—under His Protection

*Those who live in the shelter of the Most High will find rest
in the shadow of the Almighty. This I declare about the LORD:
He alone is my refuge, my place of safety; he is my God, and I trust him.*
PSALM 91:1–2 NLT

Where do you live? Where are you living right now, this instant?

If you are abiding in Christ, moment by moment, you are constantly safe under His protection. In that secret place, that hidden place in Him, you can maintain a holy serenity, a peace of mind that surpasses all understanding. If you are trusting in God, nothing can move you or harm you.

If money problems, physical illness, time pressures, job woes, the state of the world, or something else is getting you down, check your location. Where are you? Where is your mind? Where are your thoughts?

Let what the world has conditioned you to think go in one ear and out the other. Stand on the truth, the promises of God's Word. Say of the Lord, "God is my refuge! I am hidden in Christ! Nothing can harm me. In Him I trust!" Say it loud. Say it often. Say it over and over until it becomes your reality. And you will find yourself dwelling in that secret place every moment of the day.

*God, You are my refuge. When I abide in You, nothing can harm me.
Your Word is the truth on which I rely. Fill me with Your light and
the peace of Your love. It's You and me, Lord, all the way! Amen.*

Your Joyful Spirit Is Contagious

*Satisfy us in the morning with your unfailing love,
that we may sing for joy and be glad all our days.*
PSALM 90:14 NIV

Webster's dictionary defines joy as "emotion evoked by well-being, success, or good fortune." When was the last time you experienced joy? Was it last month? Last week? Today?

There are many joyful occasions: a birthday, an anniversary, a job promotion, a wedding, the birth of a baby. . .the list goes on. But do we need a big event to give us joy? Many ordinary moments can bring joy as well: getting a close parking spot at the grocery store, finding a ten-dollar bill in your pocket. . .again, the list continues.

First Thessalonians 5:16 (NLT) tells us to "always be joyful." That doesn't mean we need to take pleasure when things go wrong in life, smiling all the while. Rather, God wants us to maintain a spirit of joy, knowing that He has provided happy times and will carry us through the hard times.

Ever notice how a joyful spirit is contagious? When you're around someone who is full of joy, it's easy to find yourself sharing in that joy. Maybe you could be that person today, bringing smiles to others. When you find delight in the ordinary moments, they will catch the joy.

*Heavenly Father, I thank You for being the source of my joy. Please help me to share Your joy with those whom I come in contact with today.
Amen.*

Today, God Wants You to Know...
He Offers Just What You Need for a Victorious Life

"I will rain down bread from heaven for you. The people are to go out each day and gather enough for that day."
Exodus 16:4 niv

O ur faith is a living, breathing organism that needs to be fed every day. Christ, His Word, and His presence are our daily manna. Jesus Himself knows that we need a daily portion of Him to renew ourselves. When He faced the hungry crowds in the wilderness, He showed His concern for their welfare. In Matthew 15:32 (nkjv) Jesus says, "I have compassion on the multitude, because they have now continued with Me three days and have nothing to eat. And I do not want to send them away hungry, lest they faint on the way."

Christ is so gracious to us. He gives us "each day our daily bread," nourishment that shields us against our mood swings, unrelenting problems, and the influence of unbelievers surrounding us. This miraculous, daily intake of Christ keeps us from fainting along the way!

God has provided you with the manna you need to feed your faith. Don't go away hungry. Take your daily portion each morning, just what you need, to live the victorious life.

Christ, I come to You hungry, needing Your nourishment, Your power, to renew my faith. I stand before You ready to ingest Your presence, to feed upon Your Word, to gain the strength to survive the wilderness of this world. Amen.

Today, God Wants You to Know...

His Way Is Always Better Than Yours

> *But the Holy Spirit produces this kind of fruit in our lives:*
> *love, joy, peace, patience, kindness, goodness, faithfulness,*
> *gentleness, and self-control. There is no law against these things!*
> GALATIANS 5:22–23 NLT

We've all had those days. Frustration mounts. Resentment surfaces. Anger brews. Our day is not going according to our plan. We might as well be beating our heads against the wall. What's the problem?

Because we are human, we tend to want to rely on ourselves to fix our problems. It's a constant battle. The apostle Paul describes this wrestling match in Romans 7:19 (NIV): "For I do not do the good I want to do; but the evil I do not want to do—this I keep on doing." Paul asks in verse 24, "Who will rescue me from this body that is subject to death?" His answer? Jesus Christ!

We need to recognize the problem. Frustration, resentment, and anger are red flags. They are by-products of our sinful nature, proving that we've bypassed the help and peace God offers. We want life to go according to our plan and agenda, but God's way is so much better. Jesus came to rescue us from ourselves. He came to enable us to walk in the Spirit by yielding control to Him. Once we do that, our lives will produce the spiritual fruit God wants us to grow. It's a better way to live!

Dear Lord, help me realize when I am walking in the flesh.
May I yield to You so that I reap spiritual fruit. Amen.

He Loves You, Despite Your Shortcomings

To him who is able to keep you from stumbling and to present
you before his glorious presence without fault and with great joy.
JUDE 1:24 NIV

Who is at fault? Who is to blame? When something goes wrong at work, at home, or at church, someone is held accountable. People want to know who is responsible, who made a mistake. The ones pointing fingers of accusation don't always care about the truth as much as they do about making sure they aren't blamed for the transgression.

Ever since God confronted Adam and Eve in the Garden of Eden, we have been pointing fingers at someone else instead of taking responsibility for our own actions. Shame and fear make us want to deny we have done any wrong even when we have done so accidentally or by mistake. We value what God and other people think of us. When we are at odds with God or others over a transgression, we often become depressed.

Jesus loves us so much despite our shortcomings. He is the One who can keep us from falling—who can present us faultless before the Father. Because of this we can have our joy restored no matter what. Whether we have done wrong and denied it or have been falsely accused, we can come into His presence to be restored and lifted up. Let us keep our eyes on Him instead of on our need to justify ourselves to God or others.

Thank You, Jesus, for Your cleansing love and
for the joy we can find in Your presence. Amen.

Today, God Wants You to Know...
There Is No Greater Love Than Laying Down Your Life for Someone Else

Follow God's example, therefore, as dearly loved children and walk in the way of love, just as Christ loved us and gave himself up for us as a fragrant offering and sacrifice to God.
EPHESIANS 5:1–2 NIV

Are you living a life of love? Ephesians 5:1–2 tells us Christ loved us and gave Himself up for us. John 15:13 tells us there is no greater love than when you are willing to lay down your life for someone else.

How can you apply this to your daily life? By putting others first! Think of others' needs before you worry about yourself. Be others-minded instead of selfish. Wholeheartedly loving another person is one of the most selfless things you will ever do.

Do you love people enough to lay down your life for them? Putting others first can be difficult to do, but when we are being "imitators of God," He fills us with His Spirit and His power, and through Him we can do all things.

Dear God, show me how to love people selflessly and wholeheartedly. Help me to be willing to lay down my life for someone else if necessary. Amen.

He Makes Your Way Perfect

"He makes my way perfect."
2 Samuel 22:33 nkjv

We always want to be in the right place at the right time. Life moves in a hurry, and with it, we thrust ourselves forward into each appointment or commitment. We get frustrated when we miss a turn or mistakenly veer down a wrong road.

What if you were to choose to put a different spin on the frustration of going out of your way? You can get bent out of shape and become frustrated because of the time you feel you have lost, or you can choose to believe that God makes your way perfect and He has kept you from harm's way. What if that wrong turn that you thought cost you ten extra minutes in traffic actually kept you from a fender-bender or something worse?

Instead of feeling lost and undone, consider that perhaps this was the path you were destined to take. A series of unfortunate events or a trip down an unexpected path can lead to a positive spin on your day. Be open to taking a different route today. It could open new doors of opportunity in unexpected ways.

Father, help me to relax, trusting that You order my
steps and make my way perfect every day. Amen.

Today, God Wants You to Know...
You Need to Be Wise When Opportunities Arise

See then that ye walk circumspectly, not as fools,
but as wise, redeeming the time, because the days are evil.
EPHESIANS 5:15–16 KJV

Is your testimony something you review on a regular basis? It should be. This world is full of darkness, and God needs dedicated Christians who truly love Him to shed His light on lost souls.

Our primary desire should be to bring people to Jesus. This doesn't mean that all we ever do is talk about God, but when He gives us opportunities, we should take them. No matter what we are doing or saying, it should always honor God.

Our time on earth is limited, and we must use every minute wisely. We will give an account of all our time, whether we waste it or use it for God's glory. That is why it is so important to look often at how we measure up to God's expectations for our lives.

Jesus is our ideal. It really doesn't matter if we are better or worse than someone else. If we don't measure up to Christ, there is work to be done. We must let God work in and through us that we might wisely use the time He gives us to make a difference for Him.

Oh God, give me a desire to make every moment I have count for You.
Help me be wise in how I conduct my life.

Today, God Wants You to Know...

He Wants Your Speech to Match Your Actions

To fear the LORD is to hate evil; I hate pride and arrogance,
evil behavior and perverse speech.
PROVERBS 8:13 NIV

When we think about our fears, our minds and bodies almost always tense. Whether it's a fear of heights, spiders, public speaking, failure, or being alone, everyone has fears. In fact, it's considered perfectly natural to avoid what we fear.

Why does the Bible say we should "fear" God? In reality, to fear God is not the same as fearing the creepy-crawly spider inching up the living room wall. Instead, we fear God when we have a deep respect and reverence for Him.

Imagine that the president of the United States was paying your home a visit. The house would be extra clean, the laundry would be washed and put away, and the children would be instructed to be on their best behavior. Why? Because the visitor deserves respect.

Our lives should reflect a similar reverence for our heavenly Father every day—our souls scrubbed extra clean, sin eliminated, and love for our Creator bursting forth in joy. God wants speech and actions to match. Take time today to stand in awe of the One who deserves our greatest respect and love.

Lord, help my daily actions and speech to reflect my respect for You.
Amen.

He Desires for You to Be Wise about Your Wealth

Anyone who can be trusted in little matters can also be trusted in important matters. But anyone who is dishonest in little matters will be dishonest in important matters. If you cannot be trusted with this wicked wealth, who will trust you with true wealth?

LUKE 16:10–11 CEV

Credit cards seem like such a simple and easy way to buy all we want. Sometimes, though, plastic helps us acquire not only a bunch of stuff, but a mountain of debt as well. Good intentions can result in never-ending bills, interest charges, and minimum payments that barely chip away at the actual money owed. Buying on credit allows us to immediately fulfill our desires for things we want, but this isn't God's way. Instead, He desires us to be wise in our wealth.

When we prove to be faithful with our own finances, God will trust us with the bigger things in life. If we patiently wait for the blessings of life to come, we will reap the rewards of satisfaction, financial security, and the trust of others. Exercise godly principles by making sound financial decisions and faithfully honoring the gifts God gives.

Jesus, thank You for the rich blessings in my life. Please help me to be patient and wise with my finances. I want to be faithful with the little things so that I will be worthy of trust in the big ones. Amen.

Today, God Wants You to Know...

He Desires for You to Live by Your Faith

No man is justified by the law in the sight of God,
it is evident: for, The just shall live by faith.
GALATIANS 3:11 KJV

Our moods often dictate our actions. For instance, we schedule lunch with a friend for Saturday afternoon, but on Saturday morning we regret having made plans. Or we strategize what to accomplish on our day off but suffer from mental anemia and physical fatigue when the day arrives. So we fail to do what we had intended to do in a more enthusiastic moment.

Emotions mislead us. One day shines with promise as we bounce out of bed in song, while the next day dims in despair and we'd prefer to hide under the bedcovers. One moment we forgive; the next we harbor resentment.

The emotional roller coaster thrusts us into mood changes and affects what we do, what we say, and the attitudes that define us.

It has been said that faith is the bird that feels the light and sings to greet the dawn while it is still dark. The Bible instructs us to live by faith—not by feelings. Faith assures us that daylight will dawn in our darkest moments, affirming God's presence so that even when we fail to pray and positive feelings fade, our moods surrender to song.

Heavenly Father, I desire for my faith, not my emotions,
to dictate my life. I pray for balance in my hide-under-the-
cover days, so that I might surrender to You in song. Amen.

He Will Give Your Heart a Makeover

Do not conform to the pattern of this world,
but be transformed by the renewing of your mind.
ROMANS 12:2 NIV

Makeovers are fun. The effects of a new hairstyle, makeup, and wardrobe can be instantaneous and dramatic. Some makeovers are so good that it's almost impossible to recognize the person in the before photo. But no matter how trendy the haircut or how cute the clothes, it's always the same person underneath, and nothing can change the heart. This is the worldly formula for transformation: change what's on the outside and maybe the inside will feel better.

The Bible presents a much more effective alternative. Paul tells us that *true* transformation radiates from the inside out. The word *transformation* means "metamorphosis." This process does not happen overnight. The process of transformation begins with the attitudes of our minds. Our attitudes determine our thoughts. Our thoughts influence our actions, and our actions reveal our character.

Allow God to influence and shape your thoughts, and your character will gradually look more and more like His. Soon you won't even recognize the person you were before. Now *that's* genuine transformation.

Father, thank You that in You I am a new creature.
Continue to transform and change my character from the inside out.

You Should Never Let Go

"Hold tight to GOD, your God, just as you've done up to now."
JOSHUA 23:8 MSG

Life is the moment—the here and now—yet we spend much of our time outside of that moment worried about, focused on, and trying to figure out the next hour, the next day, week, or month. *Where will the money for this come from? Where will I be next year? How will my children turn out?*

Life comes at us fast—and we have to take each challenge as it comes. Sometimes there are so many variables to juggle that we just want to give up. Don't let go—but hold on. The enemy of your soul *wants* you to quit. You've come this far in your faith believing that God will keep His promises and help you reach your destiny.

When you don't think you can take another step—don't! Just hold on. Tomorrow will give you a fresh start with the strength you need to go a little further and hold on a little longer. Take a deep breath, get a fresh grasp on your faith, and don't let go. God will help you get to your dream.

Lord, help me to hold fast to You. With You by my side,
I can make it through all the circumstances of life no matter
how tough they seem. I trust You to help me hold on. Amen.

He Will Complete the Great Work He Started in You

Being confident of this very thing, that he which hath begun a good work in you will perform it until the day of Jesus Christ.
PHILIPPIANS 1:6 KJV

When you accepted Jesus as Savior, that was just the beginning of His work in your life. Yes, salvation was complete through His grace. Your sins were forgiven, and your home in heaven was secured.

But Christ wants so much more for you. He wants you to grow in your faith. He wants to help you flee the temptations that you will inevitably face. He wants to give you strength to be joyful even as you go through trials. His ultimate desire is to help you become more like Him.

Do you allow Jesus to be as involved in your life as He wants to be? Unfortunately, a lot of people accept Him in order to get into heaven, but then they want little more to do with Him. Why not choose now to let Him be a part of everything you do and every decision you make? Go to Him in prayer. Seek answers from His Word and from the Holy Spirit. He will do a great work in your life. He will be faithful to complete what He started in you—and you will become like Him.

Dear Jesus, thank You for wanting to help me be like You. Thank You for being involved in my life and not leaving me to my own designs.

He Will Make Your Sleep Sweet

It is vain for you to rise up early, to sit up late,
to eat the bread of sorrows: for so he giveth his beloved sleep.
PSALM 127:2 KJV

We women are funny creatures.

If we are asked if we want God's blessings, we passionately say, "Of course we do!"

Why then do we reject His gifts?

Psalm 127:3 says, for example, that children are a heritage and reward. Yet we say, "Two rewards are enough, God."

That same psalm also says that sleep is a gift. Of all God's gifts for health and prosperity that He wants to bestow on us, it's the one modern women reject without a thought.

Thanks to the lightbulb, we have options. We don't have to go to bed when the sun goes down. We can now sit up late doing anything we want.

Ignoring sleep is faithlessness. Long nights of work show that we don't trust God to provide our needs. He says, "Sleep, and I will take care of you."

Not only will God take care of us when we sleep, but He also promises new mercies each morning (Lamentations 3:23). Waking renewed is one such mercy.

Instead of vainly burning the midnight oil, be blessed: go to bed.

Thank You, Father, for giving me sleep. Let me rest in You
each night, knowing You will provide for my needs according
to Your exceedingly abundant riches in Jesus. Amen.

He Provides Wisdom for
Every Decision You Make

*Those who live only to satisfy their own sinful nature will harvest
decay and death from that sinful nature. But those who live to
please the Spirit will harvest everlasting life from the Spirit.*
GALATIANS 6:8 NLT

In decision making there is a cost factor associated with everything you do—and everything you don't do. Action and lack of
action both cost you.

Take exercise, for example. Regular physical exercise offers
amazing benefits. It strengthens your body, boosts your immune
system, and improves mental health. The cost to exercise includes
the time you need to actually do it and the pain of putting your
body through the motions to get in shape. But there is also a cost
associated with not exercising, such as deteriorating physical and
mental health.

When you make a decision, remember to take a look at the
whole picture. What will it cost you if you act? What will it cost
you if you fail to act? Everything you do—or don't do—carries
consequences.

God made wisdom available to you to help you make good
choices for your life. The next time you are faced with a decision,
take a step back and count the cost!

*Heavenly Father, thank You for making wisdom available to me.
I ask You to show me how to count the cost in all my choices. Amen.*

Today, God Wants You to Know...

Lasting Treasure Can Be Found Only in Him

> *"Beware! Guard against every kind of greed.*
> *Life is not measured by how much you own."*
> LUKE 12:15 NLT

Contrary to popular belief, material riches do not guarantee happiness. Beaming smiles often radiate from faces in third-world countries while depression soars in the lands of plenty. Many times prosperity breeds discontentment and dissatisfaction. Lottery winners have declared bankruptcy. Professional athletes have succumbed to drug abuse. Movie stars have become inmates. Greed is an insatiable appetite that destroys lives.

The Lord never meant for us to be satisfied with temporary treasures. Earthly possessions leave us empty because our hearts are fickle. Once we gain possession of one thing, our hearts yearn for something else.

Lasting treasure can be found only in Jesus Christ. He brings contentment so that the treasure chests of our souls overflow in abundance. Hope is placed in the Lord rather than our net-worth statement. Joy is received by walking with the Lord, not by chasing some fleeting fancy. Love is showered upon us as we grab hold of real life—life that cannot be bought, but that can only be given through Jesus Christ.

Jesus is enough. Jesus is everything. Find joy and contentment in Christ alone.

Dear Lord, may I be content with what You have given me. May I not wish for more material treasures but seek eternal wealth from You. Amen.

Today, God Wants You to Know...
He Honors Humble Work

Well reported of for good works; if she have brought up children, if she have lodged strangers, if she have washed the saints' feet, if she have relieved the afflicted, if she have diligently followed every good work.
1 TIMOTHY 5:10 KJV

With so many choices in today's world, what's a woman to do? What's she to do with her time and her talents?

That's a tough question, especially in this me-centered, career-driven world. Women have so many opportunities that we can get ourselves quite confused as we look at all the options.

This confusion persists in our service to God. What does *He* want me to do? Wouldn't it be better to be working with orphans in Zambia than washing dishes in suburbia?

Who knows?

God does. His Word clearly explains a woman's work. This work includes keeping house, ministering to the poor, helping those in the church, and practicing hospitality. A widow who was worthy of church support had to have done all these things.

Such work is not very glamorous. It does not garner headlines or large paychecks. It is disdained by the world and even by some in the church.

But this is the humble work God honors, the work that will one day be praised.

Dear Lord, Your Word is so clear on what You expect of me. How can I miss it? And why do I so easily reject it? Teach me contentment in my calling as a woman. Amen

Today, God Wants You to Know...

He Places People in Your Life for a Reason

*You have heard me teach things that have been confirmed by
many reliable witnesses. Now teach these truths to other
trustworthy people who will be able to pass them on to others.*
2 TIMOTHY 2:2 NLT

Whom you spend your time with says a lot about you. Time is an investment of yourself into the relationships you value most. Take a look at your inner circle—those whom you allow to know you best and speak the most into your life.

Jesus chose twelve men to trust to grow with Him and learn from Him. They asked Him questions and made choices in their own lives that had an impact on His life and His ministry. And in the same way, His answers and decisions greatly influenced them. They knew Him well, and He knew them better than they knew themselves.

It matters whom you spend time with because you usually become like those you are with the most. It's so important to choose friendships and relationships wisely and be aware of the influence that you have on others as well as their influence on you.

There are people God desires to use to help you live life with Christ at the center. Be certain those who speak into your life and help you make decisions are supporting and guiding you toward God and His design for your life.

*God, I want relationships that will bring me closer to You.
Help me to choose the healthy relationships that keep
me accountable in my daily walk with You. Amen.*

Today, God Wants You to Know...
He Has a Plan for Your Future

"What no eye has seen, what no ear has heard,
and what no human mind has conceived"—
the things God has prepared for those who love him.
1 CORINTHIANS 2:9 NIV

What if Cinderella had said no? The handsome prince breezes in, the slipper fits, but Cinderella says, "No thanks. I'd rather stay here and be doomed to a life of drudgery. It's sweet of you to want to take me away from all this, but I've grown accustomed to my little prison and I don't want to leave."

Not much of a fairy tale, is it? But when God offered the Israelites a trip to the Promised Land, they responded in much the same way. Since they couldn't see the future, they thought they'd rather continue working as slaves.

God's promise for our future is so magnificent we can't even comprehend it. He has great plans for each of us, but we often become paralyzed by fear. Why? Because the past seems more comfortable. Because the future is uncertain.

While God doesn't give us a map of what our future is like, He does promise that it will be more than we could ever ask or imagine. What steps of faith do you need to take today to accept God's glorious future for your life?

God, Your ways are not my ways and Your plans are too
wonderful for me to even comprehend. Help me never to
be satisfied with less than Your glorious plans for my life.

Today, God Wants You to Know...

What You Do Influences More Than What You Say

Now when Jesus came into the district of Caesarea Philippi, He was asking His disciples, "Who do people say that the Son of Man is?"
MATTHEW 16:13 NASB

Jesus stirred things up in His generation. His actions caused people to talk. His ministry—His love, compassion, and miracles of healing—were heard of all over the land. Many of the leaders of the day saw His popularity and influence as a threat to their position and power and tried to silence Him. Those who sought and believed in Him found healing, salvation, and a better life.

Just as people watched Jesus in His lifetime, people are watching you. What are people saying about you? What do your actions tell them about you and your relationship with God? Jesus' words and teachings were powerful, but it was His actions that caused others to stop and take notice.

What matters most isn't really what you say—it's what you do that speaks the loudest in the lives of those around you. Who do others say you are? And does what you do each day point people to Christ? Your reputation precedes you. Take inventory of your influence today.

Lord, thank You for reminding me that I represent You in everything I do. Help me to make godly choices and good decisions to influence others to see You in my life. Amen.

Today, God Wants You to Know...
He Sees Only Your Beauty

> *Behold, thou art fair, my love; behold,*
> *thou art fair; thou hast doves' eyes.*
> SONG OF SOLOMON 1:15 KJV

Getting up in the morning and looking in the mirror can be tough. The glass reflects back our exact image with all the blemishes in plain sight. In our eyes, the flaws stand out. Instead of seeing any beauty, we focus on the imperfections. The longer we consider them, the more pronounced they become. Before long, we see only ugliness in ourselves.

No matter how hard we try, when the focus is on self, we see shortcomings. Beauty treatments, plastic surgery, makeup, beautiful clothing—nothing helps. There is no way to cover the flaws we see. Our outlook even affects how others view us.

Our only hope is to see ourselves through a different mirror. We must remember that as we grow as Christians, we take on the characteristics of Christ. The more we become like Him, the more beautiful we are in our own eyes and to those around us.

When God looks at us as Christians, He sees the reflection of Christ. He sees us as very beautiful. God loves to behold us when we are covered in Christ. The mirror image He sees has none of the blemishes or imperfections, only the beauty.

Oh God, thank You for beholding me as being fair and valuable.
Help me to see myself through Your eyes. Amen.

Today, God Wants You to Know...
He Loves You Perfectly

There is no fear in love. But perfect love drives out fear, because fear has to do with punishment. The one who fears is not made perfect in love.

1 JOHN 4:18 NIV

Light dispels darkness. No matter how dark the room, turn the light on and darkness is chased away. The tightest corner cannot escape the flood of light.

Perfect love is like light. God's love for us is perfect. It is complete. The sacrifice of His Son to reconcile us to Himself is the ultimate act of this love. He came to us in our sinfulness, loving us first, so that we could love Him.

If we are so loved, why do we fear? We worry about the future: Is a job in jeopardy? A relationship rocky? Fear for our family grips us. We fear old age, poor health, or poverty. We fear rejection by others, so we say yes to more than we should. We fear failure, so we shy away from callings and responsibilities.

Perhaps it's difficult to trust God because we have not truly basked in how much He loves us. Romans 8:35–39 (NASB) says nothing can separate us from the love of God that is in Christ Jesus—not tribulation, distress, persecution, famine, nakedness, peril, or sword. Daily we need the light of His love shining into the dark corners of our mind, chasing away fear that seeks to dwell there.

Lord, help me to know more of Your deep and complete love for me.

Today, God Wants You to Know...
His Truth Will Lead You to Life

Does not wisdom cry out, and understanding lift up her voice?
She takes her stand on the top of the high hill,
beside the way, where the paths meet.
PROVERBS 8:1–2 NKJV

*W*isdom. The very term sounds outdated, a concept hiding in musty, dusty caverns of the past. Has it anything to do with real life?

Many answer, "No, especially in a new millennium!"

But biblical wisdom, crafted by God before the earth existed, remains as fresh and powerful as its Creator. In the book of Proverbs, God personifies wisdom as a godly woman who does not hesitate to let her voice be heard. She stands atop a high hill "where the paths meet," at busy intersections, trying to help travelers find their way. But they rush past Wisdom, most talking into cell phones glued to their ears. Business meetings must start on time. Carpools must follow schedules. Bills must be paid. The travelers hardly notice Wisdom as they scurry past her. Focused on themselves, they make their deadlines and achieve their goals. Most do not realize they are completely lost.

Wisdom longs to make a difference in their stressful existence that leads to destruction. She never stops sharing her vital message: whoever heeds God's instruction gains more than silver, gold, or rubies. His truth, His directions lead listeners to life.

Father, help us shake off the hypnotizing effects of our culture's
values and listen to Your wisdom. Give us courage to share
with others who desperately need Your truth. Amen.

Today, God Wants You to Know. . .

He Offers Spiritual Water for Your Soul

"But whoever drinks the water I give them will never thirst.
Indeed, the water I give them will become in them a
spring of water welling up to eternal life."
JOHN 4:14 NIV

Imagine never being thirsty again! No more water bottles or Gatorade. . . Your thirst would always be quenched.

The woman at the well in John 4 was just a little confused when Jesus offered to quench her thirst forever. She thought Jesus was talking about making her life simpler by eliminating her need to return to the well for water all the time. It took her some time, but she eventually understood. Jesus was really offering her spiritual water for her soul. She ran back to her town wondering if He was the Christ.

Jesus offers us that same spiritual water today. We come to Him for eternal life, and then He continues to fill us with His Spirit forever. When you think of your life as a Christian, are you bubbling up with love for the Lord, or are you a little dried up? Return to the well and ask Him to refill your cup.

Dear Jesus, let my life overflow with love for You. Fill me up and let others around me see the difference You make in my life. Amen.

He Provides Peace That
Passes All Understanding

Be anxious for nothing, but in everything by prayer and supplication,
with thanksgiving, let your requests be made known to God;
and the peace of God, which surpasses all understanding,
will guard your hearts and minds through Christ Jesus.

PHILIPPIANS 4:6–7 NKJV

Some days it is easy to be thankful. We nearly bubble over with thanksgiving. These are mountaintop days—a graduation day, a wedding, or a reunion with old friends. The day comes to a close, and we whisper a prayer. It flows easily off the tongue. "Thank You, God," we say, "for a perfect day."

There are days when thankfulness is not so natural, not so easy. These are valley days—in the hospital room, at the graveside, or when we are distraught about a relationship or work issue. It is in these times that the Father wants us to give Him our burdens through prayer. It seems impossible to be thankful for the pain, the confusion, or the longings in our lives. We can be thankful, though, that we have a loving heavenly Father who stands ready to help.

The peace of God cannot be explained. It cannot be bought. The world cannot give it to us. But when we release our cares to the Lord in prayer, His peace washes over us and fills our hearts and minds. What a comfort is the peace of God when we find ourselves in the valley.

Sovereign God, You are the same yesterday, today, and tomorrow.
You are with me through the good and the bad. Draw near
to me and replace my worry with Your peace. Amen.

Today, God Wants You to Know...
You Are His Masterpiece

For you created my inmost being; you knit me together in my mother's
womb. I praise you because I am fearfully and wonderfully made;
your works are wonderful, I know that full well.
PSALM 139:13–14 NIV

We women often believe we should look like the models on magazine pages. Every day we're sent messages that outward appearance is what matters most. We feel we should be stick thin—yet curvy in all the right places. If our skin isn't perfect, we can purchase the newest skin care cosmetics for a flawless, airbrushed look. We contemplate surgeries to alter our appearance. We avoid mirrors because they reveal our imperfections rather than perfect bodies.

God made your body. He designed you and knew you fully before anyone else ever laid eyes on you. And He thinks you are just right. He loves you no less and no more based upon your weight, your height, or the blemishes on your face. He sees you as His beautiful daughter, made righteous through Christ's blood that was shed for you on the cross. He sees your heart.

Praise God for the woman you are. He has great plans for you and desires to use your gifts for His purposes. Be confident in who you are!

God, enable me to see myself as Your daughter,
designed by Your hand to be exactly who I am. Amen.

Today, God Wants You to Know...
When you're at the End of Your Rope, He'll Tie a Knot

*Let us not become weary in doing good, for at the
proper time we will reap a harvest if we do not give up.*
GALATIANS 6:9 NIV

Have you ever felt that God abandoned you? Have the difficulties in your life pressed you to physical and mental exhaustion? Do you feel your labor is in vain and no one appreciates the sacrifices you have made?

When Elijah fled for his life in fear of Jezebel's wrath, depression and discouragement tormented him. Exhausted, he prayed for God to take his life, and then he fell asleep. When he awoke, God sent an angel with provisions to strengthen his weakened body. Only then was he able to hear God's revelation that provided the direction and assistance he needed.

God hears our pleas even when He seems silent. The problem is that we cannot hear Him because of physical and mental exhaustion. Rest is key to our restoration.

Just when the prophet thought he could go on no longer, God provided the strength, peace, and encouragement to continue. He does the same for us today. When we come to the end of our rope, God ties a knot. And as with Elijah, God will do great things in and through us if we will just hold on.

*Dear Lord, help me when I can no longer help myself.
Banish my discouragement and give me the rest and
restoration I need so that I might hear Your voice. Amen.*

When You Cultivate Loyalty, the World Will Take Notice

Ruth replied, "Don't urge me to leave you or to turn back from you.
Where you go I will go, and where you stay I will stay."
RUTH 1:16 NIV

Loyalty is fast becoming a dying virtue. In our fast-food, instant-message society, "stick-to-itiveness" appears quaint and old-fashioned. But God doesn't look at loyalty that way. In fact, God praises and encourages it all through the scriptures. After all, He is loyal to us—even when we are not faithful to Him.

In the book named after her, Ruth's loyalty played out as she stuck with her relative Naomi after the deaths of both their husbands. Ruth could have gone her own way, as her sister-in-law did. Naomi even begged Ruth to leave, sure that her daughter-in-law's future would not be bright with a mother-in-law in tow.

What does loyalty look like in today's world? For a wife, it could mean not gossiping about her husband when she's at dinner with her girlfriends. For an employee, loyalty might equal sticking with a struggling company because of its godly mission statement. For a church member, loyalty might mean years of faithful service in a thankless volunteer position.

If we are to be all God wants us to be, we must cultivate loyalty. And when we do, the world will notice.

Lord, I praise You for Your unshakable loyalty to me. Help me to be loyal
not only to You, but also to my family, friends, church, and employer.

You Must Be Willing to Love as He Loves

"A new command I give you: Love one another.
As I have loved you, so you must love one another."
JOHN 13:34 NIV

Tumbleweeds have a reputation of being an annoyance. They grow with little water. When they are mature, they break free of their roots in a wind and blow whichever direction the breeze takes them. They are full of little stickers that can poke into you or your car's radiator. If you walk too close to them, you can also get small, painful barbs in your skin.

One woman riding her bike had an accident and landed in the middle of a large tumbleweed. The plant was still a bit green, and she'd never seen one so close. To her amazement, in the midst of all the prickly parts were tiny, beautiful flowers. After she extricated herself, she bent close to examine the beauty she couldn't have noticed without getting close to the irascible plant.

Oftentimes people we meet in the workplace, at the store, or even in church have prickly exteriors. They grumble, complain, or are disagreeable in a number of ways. Jesus commanded us to love one another. When we take the time to get close to a person who is difficult, we can often see some small piece of beauty amid the orneriness. The willingness to love as Jesus loves is worth the risk of getting pierced by a word or an attitude.

Jesus, show me how to love the unlovable. Help me to understand
their attitude and to emulate You, not those around me. Amen.

Today, God Wants You to Know. . .
His Word Will Transform Your Thinking

"You will know the truth, and the truth will set you free."
JOHN 8:32 NLT

Have you ever believed a lie about yourself? Perhaps someone told you that you weren't beautiful, that you had no talent, or that you'd never amount to anything.

Moses was a man who believed a lie about himself. In Exodus, when God called him to lead the children of Israel, he responded that he was "slow of speech." He doubted that people would listen to him (see Exodus 3–4). However, in Acts 7:22 (NLT), Stephen says that Moses was "powerful in both speech and action." Moses certainly didn't have the same confidence in himself that God did. If he had acted on the lies he believed, he never would have been able to lead the children of Israel out of slavery.

What lies do you believe about yourself? How might those lies be preventing you from experiencing God's plan for *your* life?

The next time you're tempted to believe a lie, write it down. Then find a scripture passage that speaks truth over the situation. Write that scripture verse across the lie. Commit the truth to memory. Over time God's Word will transform your thinking and you'll begin to believe the truth. Then something amazing will happen—you'll be set free.

Father, thank You for the truth Your Word speaks about my life.
Open my eyes to the truth and help me to believe it. Amen.

He Will Prepare You for His Kingdom Work

*All Scripture is inspired by God and profitable for teaching,
for reproof, for correction, for training in righteousness; so that
the man of God may be adequate, equipped for every good work.*
2 TIMOTHY 3:16–17 NASB

Have you thought, *How am I to accomplish this work?* Have you ever felt inadequate for the task set before you?

God gives us the aptitude and ability to do the work He leads us to. However, we may find it challenging at times because God is using the tasks to draw us into a closer relationship to Him through His Word. We are told that all of God's Word, the Bible, has the purpose of teaching, admonishing, correcting or modifying our behavior, and instructing us to be right with the Lord. Regardless of the type of work, God is enabling us to do the work He has purposed for us.

Therefore, it is important that we spend time in God's Word. We are to participate in Bible studies, worship God with fellow believers, and have a daily time of prayer and devotions. It is through these activities that we will become proficient, equipped for the good work God has planned for us. God's Word tells us we can trust Him to make us capable, adequate, prepared to do the good work we are destined to do for His kingdom.

*Lord, I praise You that Your Word can mold me into
someone who is capable of carrying out Your good works.
Help me to consistently study Your Word. Amen.*

When You Call on Him, He Will Save You

For "whoever calls on the name of the LORD shall be saved."
ROMANS 10:13 NKJV

No one gets lost on purpose. It's easy to do, though—miss a turn off the freeway in an unfamiliar city, forget where you parked your car in a busy shopping mall, or lose your way off a hiking trail. The disconnect from the familiar is unsettling, and like a child separated from his mother in the grocery store, you probably call out for help.

Your spiritual journey is no different. It's a path that can seem familiar, and then a distraction—even for a moment—occurs and you find yourself in unfamiliar territory. The path seems lost, and the night grows dark. You feel alone and confused. You call out to God, but maybe for a little while you don't hear anything. You may have to listen intently for a while, but eventually you are reassured by His voice.

When He calls your name, you know you are safe. You may have to take a few steps in the dark, but by moving toward Him you eventually see clearly. A light comes on in your heart, and you recognize where you are and what you need to do to get back on the path God has set before you.

Heavenly Father, help me to stay focused on You. Show me how to remove distractions from my life so I can stay close to You. Amen.

He Expects You to Enjoy Life

A happy heart makes the face cheerful.
PROVERBS 15:13 NIV

Can you remember the last time you laughed in wild abandon? Better yet, when was the last time you did something fun, outrageous, or out of the ordinary? Perhaps it is an activity you haven't done since you were a child, like slip down a waterslide, strap on a pair of ice skates, or pitch a tent and camp overnight.

Women often become trapped in the cycle of routine, and soon we lose our spontaneity. Children, on the other hand, are innately spontaneous. Giggling, they splash barefoot in rain puddles. Wide-eyed, they watch a kite soar toward the treetops. They make silly faces without inhibition; they see animal shapes in rock formations. In essence, they possess the secret of serendipity.

A happy heart turns life's situations into opportunities for fun. For instance, if a storm snuffs out the electricity, light a candle and play games, tell stories, or just enjoy the quiet. When we seek innocent pleasures, we glean the benefits of a happy heart.

Jesus said, "I am come that they might have life, and that they might have it more abundantly" (John 10:10 KJV). God wants us to enjoy life, and when we do, it lightens our load and changes our countenance.

So try a bit of whimsy just for fun. And rediscover the secret of serendipity.

Dear Lord, because of You, I have a happy heart.
Lead me to do something fun and spontaneous today! Amen.

He Will Replace Your Anxiety with Peace

It is vain for you to rise up early, to sit up late,
to eat the bread of sorrows; for so He gives His beloved sleep.
PSALM 127:2 NKJV

Bills. Dirty dishes. Unexpected phone calls. Projects and assignments. Thing after thing, chore after chore demands your attention, day after day after very long day.

So you set your alarm clock for an hour earlier. You work through your lunch break and hurry through dinner. You stay up an hour later than you had intended. Saturday and Sunday serve as catch-up days, and then the week begins again.

Are you tiring yourself out? Do you find yourself exhausted at each day's end? To work without rest is not only physically unhealthy; it is also spiritually unhealthy. God intends for us to find a balance between work and rest. He commanded that we keep the Sabbath for just this purpose. This day should be set aside for praise and worship, certainly, but we are also to *rest*—to take quiet personal time for ourselves and to reflect upon our busy lives.

Take time for solitude, for reflection, for being still. The time spent away from your work will serve to rejuvenate you—physically, mentally, and spiritually—so that you may approach life directly and positively, as you should.

Lord, give me rest. Take my anxieties over the trivialities of life and give to me instead Your peace so that I may act graciously toward others.

Today, God Wants You to Know…

He Will Give You Confidence
for Every Challenge

"In quietness and confidence shall be your strength."
ISAIAH 30:15 NKJV

Many times we begin in confidence as we rest in the Lord, leaning on His strength. But we begin to falter when the waters rise or the wind picks up. We take our eyes off Christ, and the waves begin to take us wherever they will.

But God tells us that when we focus on and rest in Him, our confidence will keep us strong. We can be like Esther, who, put her confidence in God and garnered the courage to go before the king for the sake of her people, saying, "If I perish, I perish!" (Esther 4:16 NKJV). This lone woman had more faith in her God than the disciples in the boat who, in the midst of a terrible storm, woke Jesus and said, "Teacher, do You not care that we are perishing?" (Mark 4:38 NKJV).

These men were filled with fear because they didn't know who Jesus was. Do you? If not, learn about Him, and bolster your confidence by reading God's Word, believing it, and storing it in your heart. (Start with Isaiah 30:15!) Do it today, and you'll find yourself confidently riding on the waves of life, making the most of every opportunity!

God, I believe in You, that You can help me take on any new challenge, any opportunity You put before me. Thank You, Lord. I sail through this life, keeping my eyes on You! Amen.

Today, God Wants You to Know...
It's Okay to Be Real

Carry each other's burdens, and in this
way you will fulfill the law of Christ.
GALATIANS 6:2 NIV

Christian women wear masks. We pretend everything is great. Admitting that we have less-than-perfect lives would be humiliating. We assume that we are the only ones experiencing problems, so we remain tight-lipped and reserved. Superficial talk dominates our conversations, allowing us to hide from each other what is really going on.

The truth is that Christians are not immune to worldly pressures. Believers suffer through divorce, addictions, eating disorders, and prodigal children, not to mention loneliness and depression. Everything is not all right. When will we be honest with one another?

God's Word instructs us to carry each other's burdens. Before that can happen, walls that hinder intimacy must be torn down. Learn to be vulnerable. Embrace honesty and affirm one another with unconditional love. There is no room for judgment. We all need the Lord so that masks can come off and burdens can be unloaded. Heartfelt prayer can be a blessing as we carry each other's burdens. We become examples of Christ. Let's take off our masks and allow someone to carry our burdens.

Dear Lord, help me to be real with others. May I allow others to carry
my burdens so that I will have the privilege of carrying theirs. Amen.

Today, God Wants You to Know...
You Should Strive to Be Quick—and Slow

My dear brothers and sisters, take note of this: Everyone should be quick to listen, slow to speak and slow to become angry, because human anger does not produce the righteousness that God desires.
JAMES 1:19–20 NIV

Kindergartners learning traffic signals know that yellow means "slow down." James 1:19–20 also is a yellow light!

Have you wished, after a conversation with a friend, that you had not given that unsolicited advice? Your friend needed a listening ear, but you attempted to fix her problem instead.

Have you raced through a hectic day, only to end it by taking out your frustrations on family members or friends? Or perhaps you have borne the brunt of someone else's anger and reacted in the same manner, thus escalating the situation. Later, when tempers calmed, you found yourself regretting the angry outburst.

Too often words escape before we know what we are saying. Like toothpaste that cannot be put back in the tube, once words are spoken it is impossible to take them back. Words, whether positive or negative, have a lasting impact.

Practice being quick and slow today—quick to listen, slow to speak, slow to become angry.

God, grant me the patience, wisdom, and grace I need to be a good listener. Remind me also, Father, to use my words today to lift others up rather than tear them down. Amen.

Today, God Wants You to Know...

He Offers True Contentment for Your Soul

> *"But seek first his kingdom and his righteousness,*
> *and all these things will be given to you as well."*
> MATTHEW 6:33 NIV

What do you seek? Wealth, harmonious relationships, an impressive home, a devoted husband, a fulfilling career? The list can go on and on. We spend much time, energy, and resources chasing after what we think our hearts desire. Yet when we get what we want, are we truly content? Or do we simply pause until another tempting carrot is dangled before us?

Our Creator knows where we will find true contentment. Seeking the things of this world will never be enough. Our hearts yearn for more. Our souls search for everlasting love and inner joy. God meets our need in the person of Jesus Christ. If we attempt to fill the emptiness of our soul with anything or anyone else, it's like chasing after the wind. We will come up empty-handed and disillusioned.

Seeking His kingdom begins by entering into a relationship with our heavenly Father through the person of Jesus Christ. Accept Jesus as your Savior. Then honor Him as Lord in your daily life. Focus on God's priorities. Value people above possessions, eternal riches over earthly ones. When we seek first His kingdom and righteousness, we have obtained the most treasured possession. He will take care of the rest.

> *Dear Lord, may I have the desire to*
> *seek You above everything else. Amen.*

Today, God Wants You to Know...
He Will Help You Grow into the Woman He Created You to Be

But the fruit of the Spirit is love, joy, peace, patience, kindness, goodness, faithfulness, gentleness, self-control; against such things there is no law.
GALATIANS 5:22–23 NASB

A charm bracelet is a beautiful way to commemorate milestones or special events. A dangling baby bootie, a tiny graduation cap, a pair of wedding bells, or a palm tree from Cancun are all commonly treasured trinkets. Each tiny charm signifies a huge achievement.

We are told in Galatians that the marks of the Holy Spirit are love, joy, peace, patience, kindness, goodness, faithfulness, gentleness, and self-control. It takes constant growth, through a consistent pursuit of godliness, to acquire these character traits. It is a struggle to walk consistently in patience, always showing love and kindness to people. Self-control is another struggle all its own. These things do not come easily to most of us, and they require concentrated effort.

Consider your spiritual charm bracelet. If you had a charm to represent your growth in each of those traits, how many would you feel comfortable attaching to your bracelet in representation of that achievement? Ask your Father which areas in your Christian walk need the most growth. Do you need to develop those traits more strongly before you feel comfortable donning your bracelet?

Lord, please show me which aspects of Christian living I need to focus on in order to have the full markings of the Holy Spirit in my life. Please help me to grow into the Christian woman You call me to be. Amen.

Today, God Wants You to Know . . .
Who You Are Is a Good Indicator of Where Your Heart Is

For where your treasure is, there will your heart be also.
MATTHEW 6:21 KJV

When others look at you, what kind of woman do you want them to see? There may be many things you would wish to include in the list of adjectives that describe you. Maybe you aren't yet who you want to be, but you know you are a work in progress. Whatever the case, who you are is a very good indication of where your heart is.

For example, your attitude about your career is something people notice. Are you driven to succeed in order to obtain a high position or salary? There's nothing wrong with desiring to succeed as long as you give God the glory and maintain a godly testimony. In fact, God could use a lot more God-fearing people running businesses and managing His finances.

If, however, you are willing to compromise God's standards in order to obtain position or wealth, your heart is not where it belongs. It is set on corruptible things that won't last but that might destroy you if your attitude goes too far in the wrong direction.

Think about where your heart is in every decision you make. Ensure it is with those incorruptible things that matter. And as you direct your heart toward God, you will become the kind of woman He wants you to be.

Oh Lord, give me wisdom to direct my heart
to lasting treasure that will honor You.

Today, God Wants You to Know. . .
He Is Your BFF

There are "friends" who destroy each other,
but a real friend sticks closer than a brother.
PROVERBS 18:24 NLT

In today's world we use the term *friend* loosely. Unable to describe a hypothetical, indefinable somebody, we often say, "I have a friend who. . ." The person usually is a distant acquaintance, but because we are unable to determine what to call them, we clump them into the multifaceted category of friend.

An ancient proverb, however, captures the essence and beauty of true friendship. It says, "Ah, the beauty of being at peace with another, neither having to weigh thoughts or measure words, but spilling them out just as they are, chaff and grain together, certain that a faithful hand will keep what is worth keeping and, with a breath of kindness, blow the rest away."

Friends find the good in us and dismiss the rest. We can be ourselves in their presence and not worry about misunderstandings or saying the wrong thing.

Jesus is that kind of friend. He sticks close by us at our most undesirable, least lovable moments. We can tell Him anything and He understands. In fact, He knows everything about us and loves us anyway. Like a true friend, Jesus enhances our good qualities and, with a breath of kindness, blows the rest away.

Dear Jesus, thank You for loving me even when I fail, encouraging me
in my discouragement, and sticking close to me during tough times.
May I be as good a friend as You are. Amen.

Today, God Wants You to Know...
You Honor Him When You
Meet Him in a Special Place

After sending them home, he went up into the hills by himself to pray.
Night fell while he was there alone.
MATTHEW 14:23 NLT

Jesus gave us a perfect example of prayer to follow. Not only can we learn *how* to pray from the Lord's Prayer, but we can also discover *where* to pray.

Although there is no magical place where we need to be to talk with Him, we should find a quiet, secluded location. He wants us to focus our thoughts on Him only—not the television program coming on in fifteen minutes, the ringing telephone, or the household chores that need to be done—just God and God alone.

Look again at the verse above. Jesus went up into the hills. You certainly don't need to go that far—although it can be an option—but your place of prayer should be free of distractions. Night fell while Jesus was there, indicating that it wasn't a hurried time of prayer. He took the time to commune with His Father, giving Him priority.

We can pray at any time, in any place, but it will benefit you and honor God when you follow Jesus' example and find a special place to talk with Him.

Lord, thank You that You listen to me anytime I come to You.
Help me to find someplace that can be for just You and me,
where I can pour out my heart to You. Amen.

His Goodness and Love
Can Rekindle Your Faith

"As your days, so shall your strength be."
DEUTERONOMY 33:25 NKJV

The morning star is a bright light that appears in the eastern sky just before sunrise. It is a sign that the darkness is nearly over and daybreak is on its way. It offers hope and encouragement to weary travelers who pressed on through the night to reach their destination and were beginning to feel that perhaps they had lost their way.

There are times in life when we feel that the night season we're facing will last forever and a new morning will never come. During that time, dreams have faded and hope is dim. We look for a flicker of encouragement, holding tightly to any sign that the night will soon pass.

For those particularly dark seasons of your life, you don't have to look to the east to find the morning star, but instead can find that morning star in your heart. Allow the hope of God's goodness and love to rekindle faith. With the passing of the night, gather your strength and courage. A new day is dawning and with it new strength for the journey forward. All that God has promised will be fulfilled.

*Heavenly Father, help me to hold tightly to faith,
knowing in this situation that daybreak is on its way. Amen.*

Today, God Wants You to Know...
He Is Waiting for Your Praise Today!

Oh, magnify the LORD with me, and let us exalt His name together.
PSALM 34:3 NKJV

It's so wonderful when people say nice things about you. It puts a smile on your face when someone notices you or the things you do. We all enjoy a word of encouragement and a little praise now and then. It takes a little thought to say something good about someone else, but it's worth it and much appreciated when it's heartfelt.

Now imagine how it must make God feel when you say good things about Him. He has given so much to us. He created a world for us and then gave His only Son to repair the breach between us and Him so we could have a relationship with Him.

There are so many ways to praise Him. Tell Him how much He means to you and how thankful you are for all He's done for you. Brag on Him to others in your life—sharing His goodness and love with them and expressing how faithful He's been to you. God's goodness makes it easy to find good things to say about Him. Make time to praise Him today!

Dear heavenly Father, I could never say enough good things about You, but I want to try. I am thankful for Your mercy and unfailing love. Your goodness is endless, and the way You express Your love to me is without measure. Thank You, Lord. You're awesome. Amen.

He Desires an Intimate Relationship with You

And now, little children, abide in him; that, when he shall appear,
we may have confidence, and not be ashamed before him at his coming.
1 JOHN 2:28 KJV

Someday each one of us will stand before our Maker. It is difficult to imagine how we will react. Will we run to Him with open arms or shrink back with embarrassment? Will we desire to sit at His feet or retreat to a far-off corner of heaven? Our reaction then will depend on our relationship with Him now.

We have the opportunity to enter into a personal relationship with our heavenly Father through Jesus Christ. The acceptance of this invitation by faith assures us of eternal life. Yet many people who profess faith in Jesus never grow in their relationship with Him. They stick their ticket to heaven in their back pocket, never realizing there is so much more!

Jesus came to give us eternal life in heaven as well as abundant life on earth. As we allow His Word to speak to our hearts, we grow in our relationship with Him. He becomes our friend, our confidant, our Good Shepherd. We know Him intimately. We communicate with Him constantly. We love Him deeply. Let's get to know the Lord now. Then we will anticipate our face-to-face meeting with excitement and confidence!

Dear Lord, help me to pursue my relationship with You now.
May I know You more with each passing day so that I
will be excited when we meet face-to-face. Amen.

Today, God Wants You to Know...
He Can Change Your Perspective on Life

Turn my eyes away from worthless things;
preserve my life according to your word.
PSALM 119:37 NIV

Read a few greeting cards targeting women, and you will soon get the message: most things can be fixed with chocolate or shopping. Pick up a magazine and learn what fashion purchases will transform your size and shape or how a spa weekend can change your outlook on life. The media and the mall are full of answers before we even ask ourselves the questions. Underneath the slick pages are messages that we deserve whatever we want and that the accumulation of possessions will fulfill us.

The book of Psalms offers hundreds of verses that can easily become sentence prayers. "Turn my eyes from worthless things" whispered before heading out to shop, turning on the television, or picking up a magazine can turn those experiences into opportunities to see God's hand at work in our lives. He can change our perspective. He will show us what has value for us. He can even change our appetites, causing us to desire the very things He wants for us. When we pray this prayer, we are asking God to show us what He wants for us. He knows us and loves us more than we know and love ourselves. We can trust His love and goodness to provide for our needs.

Father, imprint this scripture in my mind today.
In moments of need, help me remember to pray
this prayer and to relinquish my desires to You.

Today, God Wants You to Know...
You Can Rest Secure in His Love

"Your kingdom come, your will be done, on earth as it is in heaven."
MATTHEW 6:10 NIV

We pray it. We say it. But do we really mean that we want God's will to be done on earth as it is in heaven? Submitting to God's will is difficult. Jesus struggled with submission in the Garden of Gethsemane. We wrestle with it most days. Unfortunately, most of us assume that we know best. We want to call the shots and be in control. But following God's path requires trusting Him, not ourselves.

Many times submitting to God's will requires letting go of something we covet. We may be called to walk away from a relationship, a job, or a material possession. At other times God may ask us to journey down a path we would not have chosen. Venturing out of our comfort zone or experiencing hardship is not our desire.

Embracing God's love enables us to submit to His will. God not only loves us immensely, but He desires to bless us abundantly. However, from our human perspective, those spiritual blessings may be disguised. That is why we must cling to truth. We must trust that God's ways are higher than ours. We must believe that His will is perfect. We must hold fast to His love. As we do, He imparts peace to our hearts, and we are able to say with conviction, "Your will be done."

Dear Lord, may I rest secure in Your unconditional love. Enable me to trust You more. May I desire that Your will be done in my life. Amen.

There's No Such Thing as Harmless Gossip

*Though some tongues just love the taste of gossip, those who
follow Jesus have better uses for language than that.*
EPHESIANS 5:3 MSG

Our tongues can sing the highest praises of someone or destroy them—all in the matter of a few seconds. And once those negative words slip past our lips, there is no way to erase them, no matter how much we wish we could.

Have you ever been a victim of gossip? It hurts when we hear what someone has said about us! The words can tear us up inside. A close friendship can easily be ruined as a result of breaking a trust.

One more question to consider: Have you ever spread gossip? You may have thought it harmless, perhaps even sharing it only as a "prayer request." However, the words you spoke may have injured someone deeply. Before speaking, take a moment to consider whether what you are about to say would be considered gossip or not. Those few seconds could spare a lifetime of grief!

If we have given our life to Jesus, our whole body is His— including the tongue. Commit it to Him, and ask Him to help you to control the words that come from your mouth. Remember, "Those who follow Jesus have better uses for language than [gossip]."

*Dear heavenly Father, please guard my tongue so I won't be
guilty of spreading gossip. Help me to seek forgiveness if I have,
and to be forgiving when gossip is spread about me. Amen.*

Today, God Wants You to Know...

He Can Help You Find Balance in the Busyness of Life

Hope deferred makes the heart sick,
but when the desire comes, it is a tree of life.
PROVERBS 13:12 NKJV

Our minds are full of the things we are trying to fix in our lives—strained relationships, financial worries, stress, health concerns.

Too much too fast is overwhelming. Looking for balance can leave us lost, not knowing which way to turn. The best way to gain balance is to stop moving and regain focus.

Jesus is your hope! He stands a short distance away bidding you to take a walk on water—a step of faith toward Him. Disregarding the distractions can be hard, but the rough waters can become silent as you turn your eyes, your thoughts, and your emotions to Him.

You can tackle the tough things as you maintain your focus. Let Him direct you over the rough waters of life, overcoming each obstacle one opportunity at a time. Don't look at the big picture in the midst of the storm, but focus on the one thing you can do at the moment to help your immediate situation—one step at a time.

Lord, help me not to concentrate on the distractions, but to keep my focus on which step to take next in order to reach You. Amen.

His Word Is Life-Giving

For the word of God is alive and active. Sharper than any
double-edged sword, it penetrates even to dividing soul and spirit,
joints and marrow; it judges the thoughts and attitudes of the heart.
HEBREWS 4:12 NIV

The world is filled with books on every topic and in many languages. You can find pages at your fingertips on a computer keyboard and can explore volumes of information that provide you with entertainment and knowledge, but only the Bible—the Word of God—can truly speak to you.

No matter what you are facing, there is always something in the Bible to help you find your way. There is simply no other book like it. Other books can encourage, inspire, and motivate—but the Bible gives life. The Word of God can infuse you with strength, sustain you in battle, and uphold you during the darkest days you'll ever face.

Maybe for you the fire of God's Word starts out as a small glowing ember. You could read for days, and then suddenly you stumble upon that scripture—those amazing words—written so many years ago that seem written specifically to you. You know it the moment the Word comes alive as it ignites your heart. It comforts you, provides an answer to the questions you've been asking, and consumes you with a hunger for the truth.

Lord, I want to read Your Word and hear Your voice as it speaks to me.
Ignite me with a passion for the Bible. Amen.

You Can Find Your Identity in Him

Charm can be deceiving, and beauty fades away,
but a woman who honors the LORD *deserves to be praised.*
PROVERBS 31:30 CEV

"Identity crisis" is a term used to describe a person who is suffering stress or anxiety over her role in society or how she is viewed by others. The world places much superficial value on charm, beauty, and feminine wiles. Scripture, however, makes it clear that those things will fade away.

Some people interpret Proverbs 31:30 as meaning that the charm of a cunning woman can be deceiving to others. But the original Hebrew wording gives a fuller picture of what is actually being taught in this verse. The warning is not that charm is deceiving to *others*; it is that it is deceiving to *you*! When you trust in something that will fade away, such as charm or beauty, you have deceived yourself into a false sense of security.

As a believer in Christ, your identity is that you are a child of the King, an heir to the kingdom of God, and a part of the body of Christ. You are His. Let that identity solve your crisis, and from now on, place no more value on your charm or beauty than He does. Your Father sees you through the blood of His Son, Jesus, and He finds you perfect.

Thank You, Jesus, for my true identity. Please help me to remember not to get caught up in the unimportant things that will fade away, but to nurture the parts of me that bring glory to You. Amen.

Today, God Wants You to Know...
He Longs for You to Release Your Worries to Him

"Look at the birds of the air; they do not sow or reap or store away in barns, and yet your heavenly Father feeds them. Are you not much more valuable than they? Can any one of you by worrying add a single hour to your life?"
MATTHEW 6:26–27 NIV

God loves you so much. You are His precious daughter, created in His image. He longs for you to find rest in Him. Over and over in His Word He reminds you that you need not worry. He calls you to cast your cares upon Him because He cares for you. He offers a special peace that the world cannot give. He vows that He has plans to prosper and not to harm you. He says you are His sheep and He is the Good Shepherd. He does not want you to worry.

Worry is a human thing. It is not of God. As Matthew 6:27 points out, worry cannot add a single hour to one's life. It is, in other words, pointless and a waste of time.

Rest right now. Still your mind and heart before God. Consciously release to Him all the worries that you cling to so tightly. Ask your Father to take care of you as He does the birds of the air and the flowers of the fields. He made you. He knows just what you need.

When your mind begins to race, remember that God has you in the palm of His hand. Worry not. God is good.

Father, take the worries that I am burdened by today. Give me rest.

All Things Are New through Your Salvation

Do not rejoice over me, my enemy; when I fall, I will arise;
when I sit in darkness, the LORD will be a light to me.
MICAH 7:8 NKJV

Past mistakes and failures are like dried pits in the bottom of a bowl of cherries. As you enjoy the fresh fruit of your life in Christ, there are times when you reach into the bowl and touch a dried, dead seed of the past.

The truth is that God has made all things new through your salvation. You may be challenged with the consequences that remain from past life choices, but God is busy turning past mistakes into future successes.

The enemy of your soul wants you to consider each failure and dwell on the past, fully intending to rob you of your future. But God wants you to take that seed of hope that seems to have died and bury it in His garden of truth—trusting Him for a new harvest of goodness and mercy.

Once you have buried that seed deep in the ground of God's love, it will grow and become a part of His destiny for your life. Maybe you have fallen and spilled a bowl of your dreams. Pick them up and plant them in God's love. Over time you will have a harvest of goodness, and your enemy will have no reason left to celebrate.

Lord, help me not to focus on the past but
to look to You every step of the way. Amen.

Today, God Wants You to Know...
He Will Free You from Your Past

*For the Lord is the Spirit, and wherever
the Spirit of the Lord is, there is freedom.*
2 CORINTHIANS 3:17 NLT

We are free in so many ways because of what Christ did for us on the cross: free from death, free from sin, free from guilt, free from shame—and the list goes on. If you have ever felt trapped by someone or something in your life and then were set free, you know that amazing feeling of relief!

That is how living our lives through Christ should feel each day. Freedom reigns in Christ. We can breathe again.

Your past doesn't have to haunt you anymore. The Lord can use it to help change the life of someone else, so don't be ashamed anymore. You are truly free. John 8:36 (NIV) says, "If the Son sets you free, you will be free indeed."

If you are still struggling with thoughts of guilt and shame, ask the Lord to free you from your past, and begin to live a life where freedom reigns!

*Dear Jesus, thank You for taking away my sin and making me free.
Help me to live like I believe that. Amen.*

Today, God Wants You to Know...
Extraordinary Things Can Happen in the Everydayness of Life

When Aquila and Priscilla had heard, they took him unto them, and expounded unto him the way of God more perfectly.
ACTS 18:26 KJV

Priscilla and Aquila, a Jewish couple, moved to Corinth and met the apostle Paul, a man who would change their lives. The three shared the same vocation: tent making. They began to work together. As they cut, stitched, and sold their wares, Paul followed Jesus' revolutionary pattern of teaching women, instructing both Aquila and Priscilla. These close friends sailed with him to Ephesus. When Paul had to leave, he trusted Priscilla and Aquila to nurture the fledgling church there.

When Apollos, a follower of John the Baptist, began to speak in an Ephesian synagogue, the couple took him home for dinner. Together, husband and wife shared the full gospel with Apollos and helped him grow spiritually. Apollos became a strong advocate for Jesus Christ and helped spread the gospel.

Priscilla's challenging life reminds us that we can grow spiritually and share our faith amid business deals, meals, and meetings. In the everydayness of life, God does extraordinary things!

Lord Jesus, thank You that Priscilla thought outside the box.
You used her to fan the flame of the Spirit in the early church.
Please use me as well. Amen.

He Will Complete All Things Concerning You

*The LORD will perfect that which concerns me; Your mercy, O LORD,
endures forever; do not forsake the works of Your hands.*
PSALM 138:8 NKJV

From childhood we are taught to finish what we start. This is an important part of our maturity. Yet as adults we all have our list of unfinished projects. There are New Year's resolutions, diets, and home improvement projects that we never quite complete. We have dreams we haven't accomplished and goals we've yet to meet. More importantly, we have attitudes and habits we need to change and sins we continue to commit. It's easy to look at what we have not done and become discouraged.

The psalmist offers hope when he tells us the Lord will complete things that concern us. We are the work of His hands and He has enduring mercy toward our failures. He is as active in our sanctification as He is in our salvation. Philippians 1:6 (NKJV) says, "Being confident of this very thing, that He who has begun a good work in you will complete it until the day of Jesus Christ." The power to change or to see difficult things through to the end comes from the Lord who promises to complete the work He begins.

*Lord, remind me of this word when I am discouraged by my lack
of progress. Help me remember Your eternal love and mercy to me.
Give me confidence that You will complete me.*

You Please Him When You Are Bold, Passionate, and Faithful

"For even if the mountains walk away and the hills fall to pieces, my love won't walk away from you, my covenant commitment of peace won't fall apart." The God who has compassion on you says so.
ISAIAH 54:10 MSG

We live in a scary world. The daily news warns of global warming, terrorist attacks, earthquakes, and hurricanes. Anxiety is a very real part of our human journey, and fear can easily cloud our view of God and distort our perspective. If we're not careful, we can dissolve into frightened, anxious women who rarely take risks or initiate new adventures.

However, God doesn't want us to live isolated, dull lives. His Word encourages us to be bold, passionate, and faithful. *Yikes,* we think. *I'm scared to go out in the city at night by myself. How can I venture out in a dangerous world without fear?*

The answer is love. All through the scriptures, God assures us of His constant, comprehensive love for us. He promises in Isaiah that even if our world literally caves in, as it has for people who have endured natural disasters, He will never walk away.

Because of His compassion for His frail children, He has a commitment to give us peace. And if we take Him at His word, we will be filled with confidence and inner peace. That kind of peace comes from knowing that we are deeply, eternally cared for—whatever happens.

Lord, thank You for Your love and Your covenant commitment of peace for me. Help me to take You at Your word.

Today, God Wants You to Know...
It's Important to Be Still Sometimes

> *"Be still, and know that I am God."*
> PSALM 46:10 NIV

From the minute the alarm clock goes off in the morning, we are busy. Many women rush off to work or begin their tasks around the house without even eating breakfast. Most of us keep hectic schedules, and it is easy to let the day pass by without a moment of peace and quiet.

In Psalm 46:10 the command to *be still* is coupled with the result of *knowing that He is God*. Could it be that in order to truly recognize God's presence in our lives, we must make time to quiet ourselves before Him?

Sitting quietly before the Lord is a discipline that requires practice. Just as in our earthly relationships, learning to be a good listener as we converse with our heavenly Father is important. If prayer remains one-sided, we will miss out on what He has to say to us.

Although God may not speak to us in an audible voice, He will direct our thinking and speak to our hearts. Stillness allows us to dwell on God's sovereignty, His goodness, and His deep love for us. He wants us to remember that He is God and that He is in control, regardless of our circumstances.

Be still. . .and know that He is God.

God, so often I do all the talking. Quiet me before You now.
Speak to my heart, I pray. Amen.

Today, God Wants You to Know...
His Word Applies to Your Everyday Life

My son, if you accept my words and store up my commands
within you. . .then you will understand the fear of
the LORD and find the knowledge of God.
PROVERBS 2:1, 5 NIV

In an age of electronic communication, isn't it a joy to receive a letter in the mail? Letters are especially sweet when they come from someone who loves us. In the Bible, King Solomon wrote a wonderful letter to his sons. We call it the book of Proverbs, but at its core, this little gem is a heartfelt love letter from a father to his sons—not only from Solomon to his sons, but from God to us.

Proverbs contains an abundance of short and sweet sayings as relevant to us now as they were to Solomon's sons centuries ago. The wisdom of Proverbs can apply to every area of our lives. It addresses everything from relationships to our finances and our work habits.

"The righteous choose their friends carefully" (Proverbs 12:26 NIV).

"The greedy bring ruin to their households" (Proverbs 15:27 NIV).

"Commit to the LORD whatever you do, and he will establish your plans" (Proverbs 16:3 NIV).

These aren't guarantees; they are timeless truths, guidelines for living, ways to increase your chances of success in life—biblical success: righteousness, integrity, honesty, wisdom that's yours for a lifetime.

Father, thank You for the wisdom found in the book of Proverbs. Amen.

Today, God Wants You to Know...

When You Have a Thankful Heart, It Blesses Him Greatly

*"Give thanks to God. . . . Shout to the nations, tell them
what he's done, spread the news of his great reputation!"*
ISAIAH 12:3 MSG

Common courtesy grows more uncommon in our society with the passing of each generation. Finding someone who puts others first and uses words like *please* and *thank you* is like finding a rare gem. Most people hurry to their next task while giving little thought to others who cross their paths.

Every favor and earthly blessing that we experience is given to us by God. It is nothing we have accomplished in our own right. All that God has done since the beginning of creation, He did for humankind. You are His greatest treasure.

Give thanks to God today for giving you life—the very air you breathe. He has given you the ability to make a living, to feed your family, and to give to others. He is a good Father—He won't withhold anything good from you.

What has God done for you lately? What doors of opportunity has He opened? Give Him the credit, tell others of His goodness, and thank Him! It blesses God to hear you express your gratitude, and it will do your heart good as well.

*God, I am thankful for all You have given me and for who
You made me to be. Help me to have a grateful heart and
to express my appreciation to You in everything! Amen.*

You Are Never Forgotten and Never Alone

The LORD will keep you from all harm—
he will watch over your life; the LORD will watch over
your coming and going both now and forevermore.

PSALM 121:7–8 NIV

When we sit in a worship service or read the Bible in private study, it is easy to think about God. But often in the activity of our day, we forget about Him. Though His presence is always with us, we are unaware of it. We move through our days sometimes without a single thought of God, yet our heavenly Father never forgets about us. He cannot; we are His children, belonging to Him through Christ.

Our lives are like an ancient city contained within walls. In an ancient city, the gatekeeper's job was to make decisions about what went in and out of the city. God is the gatekeeper of our lives. He is always watching, always guarding, and ever vigilant in His care of us, even when we are least aware that He is doing so.

Proverbs 2:8 (NKJV) says, "He guards the paths of justice, and preserves the way of His saints." By sending His Son to save us and His Spirit to dwell in us, He has assured us that we are never forgotten and never alone.

Forgive me, Father, for how often I forget about You.
Help me remember that You are guarding and preserving me
and that nothing comes into my life without Your permission.

He Will Make Your Paths Straight

*Trust in the L*ORD *with all your heart and lean not on your*
own understanding; in all your ways submit to him,
and he will make your paths straight.
PROVERBS 3:5–6 NIV

Our knowledge is limited. As hard as we try to figure things out, our wisdom is finite. We cannot see the future. We cannot grasp how today's events will affect tomorrow. We are not God. If we lean on our own understanding, we will invariably make wrong decisions that lead to dead-end roads.

God rarely reveals what tomorrow has in store. Instead, He chooses to light our path today so that we must trust Him for tomorrow. As we trust Him moment by moment, He shines light on our next step. He enables us to navigate one step at a time as He reveals pitfalls and prevents us from stumbling. His light helps us traverse the steepest mountains and deepest valleys—one step at a time.

Do you feel as though you've been going around and around in circles? Or perhaps you find yourself on a dead-end road. Cry out to Jesus, the light of the world. He wants to lead you down a wonderful path for your life. Trust Him with all your heart. He will shine His light and show you the way. Acknowledge Him. He will make your paths straight.

Dear Lord, please make my paths straight
as I trust You with all my heart. Amen.

Today, God Wants You to Know. . .
He Desires to Hear from You Each Morning

*Why art thou cast down, O my soul? and why art
thou disquieted in me? hope thou in God: for I shall yet
praise him for the help of his countenance. O my God, my soul
is cast down within me: therefore will I remember thee from
the land of Jordan, and of the Hermonites, from the hill Mizar.*
PSALM 42:5–6 KJV

It's easy for life's responsibilities and commitments to drag us
down. Each day seems like a repeat of the day before. The morning alarm becomes our enemy, and the snooze button becomes our
considerate companion. Our hard work often goes unappreciated.
Nothing feels accomplished. Our souls yearn for something more.

If we accept it, God's constant goodness can be our delight.
In the mornings, instead of our groaning and hiding beneath the
pillows, God desires for us to communicate with Him. His voice
could be the first one that we hear each day. As we roll over and
stretch, we can then say, "I love you, God. Thank You for another
day of life."

Our willingness to speak with God at the day's beginning
shows our dependence on Him. We can't make it alone. It is a
comforting truth that God never intended for us to trek through
the hours unaccompanied. He promises to be with us. He also
promises His guidance and direction as we meet people and receive
opportunities to serve Him.

Getting started is as simple as removing our heads from beneath the pillows and telling God good morning.

Lord, refresh my spirit and give me joy for today's activities. Amen.

Today, God Wants You to Know...

He Can Help You Live Every Day with Your Eyes on Eternity

"In this world you will have trouble.
But take heart! I have overcome the world."
JOHN 16:33 NIV

Images on television sometimes convince us that evil triumphs over good. War. Hunger. Poverty. Domestic disputes. Random acts of violence. Drugs.

Seeing the world's brokenness can leave us discouraged. And we Christians do not find ourselves immune from that brokenness. Divorce, racism, and greed pervade our congregations as they do our communities. Some days it is hard to see the difference between how the world lives and how we live: in fear.

This should not be. Christ tells us to hold on to the hope we have in Him. He tells us to *"take heart"* because the trials of this world have already been won, the evil has already been conquered, and He has already overcome the world. Do you live your life as though you trusted His words, or do you live in doubt?

Live your life as a statement of hope, not despair. Live with your eye on eternity, not the here and now. Daily remind yourself that you serve a powerful and gracious God, and decide to be used by Him to act as a messenger of grace and healing to the world's brokenness.

Lord, forgive my doubts. Forgive me for growing discouraged
and not placing my full trust in You. May I learn to trust
You better and to live my life as a statement of hope.

He Will Help Soothe Your Hurts and the Hurts of Others

A man has joy in an apt answer, and how delightful is a timely word!
PROVERBS 15:23 NASB

Hurts often are soothed with the rich love found in our relationships with others. When a friend faces disappointment, we naturally want to make it better for her. A wonderful way to do that is to offer comfort—an understanding smile, a warm hug, or a few words of affirmation. Maybe she just needs someone who will listen as a gesture of support.

Comfort is not counsel. A friend may not be looking to us to solve the problem or offer advice. She may simply need a shoulder to cry on, a hand to hold, and a heart that desires to understand. She is looking for a strong spiritual relationship with a friend she can trust.

Comfort is God's cure for disappointment. Maybe we don't understand exactly what a friend is going through, but we can offer comfort by being honest—letting them know we have never experienced their situation, but we are there to walk with them through the storm and hold them up when they feel weak.

Lord, help me to be aware of the needs of others and help me to find the words to reach out to them. Amen.

He Can Get the Attention of Saints and Cynics Alike

*For ever since the world was created, people have seen the
earth and sky. Through everything God made, they can
clearly see his invisible qualities—his eternal power and
divine nature. So they have no excuse for not knowing God.*

ROMANS 1:20 NLT

You can see the love of Jesus in the eyes of a newborn baby.
You can see the paintbrush of God in the colors of a sunset.
It is awe inspiring to look at the handiwork of God and attempt
to grasp His majesty and incredible creativity. For a Christian, it's
impossible to see His creation and deny His existence.

There are skeptics and cynics, though. They love to question
the possibility of a divine Creator. They have seemingly sound
arguments based in logic and science. We can share testimonials,
blessings, and miracles from our personal lives and from scripture.
But these are often met with disbelief and tales of big bangs and
evolution.

In order for skeptics to be changed to seekers, Jesus must grab
their attention, often using His children to do that. Take time
to really consider the miraculous works of God that prove His
existence. Pray for wisdom and compelling words to lead cynics to
the throne.

*Father, help me to be a good witness of
You and Your miraculous wonders.*

Today, God Wants You to Know...

It Will Always Be Worth the Wait

Every good and perfect gift is from above, coming down from the Father
of the heavenly lights, who does not change like shifting shadows.
James 1:17 NIV

Do you know a true gift giver? We all give gifts on birthdays and at Christmas, when we receive wedding invitations, and when a baby is born. But do you know someone with a real knack for gift giving? She finds all sorts of excuses for giving gifts. She delights in it. A true gift giver has an ability to locate that "something special." When shopping for a gift, she examines many items before making her selection. She knows the interests and preferences, the tastes and favorites of her friends and family members. She chooses gifts they will like—gifts that suit them well.

God is a gift giver. He is, in fact, the Creator of all good gifts. He finds great joy in blessing you. The God who made you certainly knows you by name. He knows your tastes and preferences. He even knows your favorites and your dreams. Most important, God knows your needs.

So in seasons of waiting in your life, rest assured that gifts chosen and presented to you by the hand of God will be worth the wait.

God, sometimes I am anxious. I want what I want, and I want it now.
Calm my spirit and give me the patience to wait for Your perfect gifts.
Amen.

CONTRIBUTORS

Scripture Index

OLD TESTAMENT